The Politics of
Reform in Ghana, 1982-1991

Written under the auspices of the
Center of International Studies, Princeton University

The Politics of Reform in Ghana, 1982-1991

Jeffrey Herbst

UNIVERSITY OF CALIFORNIA PRESS
Berkeley · Los Angeles · Oxford

University of California Press
Berkeley and Los Angeles, California

University of California Press, Ltd.
Oxford, England

© 1993 by
The Regents of the University of California

Library of Congress Cataloging-in-Publication Data

Herbst, Jeffrey Ira.
    The politics of reform in Ghana, 1982–1991 / Jeffrey Herbst.
        p.   cm.
    Includes index.
    ISBN 0-520-07752-0 (alk. paper). — ISBN 0-520-07753-9 (pbk. :
alk. paper)
        1. Ghana—Economic policy.   2. Ghana—Politics and
government—1979–   3. Africa—Politics and government—1960–
4. Africa—Economic policy.   I. Title.
    HC1060.H47   1993
    338.9667—dc20   92-3297
                                                                   CIP

Printed in the United States of America
1   2   3   4   5   6   7   8   9

The paper used in this publication meets the minimum requirements of
American National Standard for Information Sciences—Permanence of Paper
for Printed Library Materials, ANSI Z39.48-1984. ∞

For Sharon

Contents

Acknowledgments

The current attempts at economic and political reform in Africa will determine whether the next generation of citizens in the countries south of the Sahara live in even greater impoverishment than before or if they can at least glimpse a brighter future. Thus, the attempts at drastic reform in Ghana—once seen as the paradigmatic African "basket case"—attracted my attention as a possible guide for the future of the continent. I was fortunate to receive a Robert S. McNamara Postdoctoral Fellowship from the World Bank to carry out research in Ghana during 1989 and 1990. Further research trips to Ghana were sponsored by the U.S. Agency for International Development as part of its project on Policy Reform in Africa (contract no. AFR-0438-C-00-9058-00) and the U.S. Information Agency. The views in this book are solely my own and should not be attributed to any of these organizations.

In Ghana, I was a research scholar in the Department of Political Science at the University of Ghana, Legon. I am especially grateful to my colleagues Dr. E. Gyimah-Boadi, Professor K. Foulson, and Dr. Kwame Ninsin for their collegiality. My thanks also to the literally hundreds of Ghanaians who consented to interviews, provided information, or pointed out new approaches to the problems I was examining. As promised, I have respected the confidentiality of my respondents.

While in Princeton, I again benefited from the support provided by the university and my colleagues. This research could not have been conducted without Princeton's generous leave policy. Nancy Bermeo, Henry Bienen, Forrest Colburn, and John Waterbury all read earlier versions of this manuscript. Their comments were a tremendous help. I am also grateful to Ms. Elizabeth Hart for her valuable research assistance. Finally, Princeton's librarians—especially Sally Burkman, Laird Klinger, Rosemary Little, Denise Shorey, and Susan White—once again provided extraordinary service without fail.

I also benefited from a conference on reform in Ghana held at The Johns Hopkins Nitze School of Advanced International Studies in 1990. An earlier version of chapter 8 was presented at the annual meeting of the African Studies Association in 1989, and parts of chapter 6 were presented at the annual meeting of the American Political Science Association in 1990. I am also grateful to many of my North American colleagues including J. Clark Leith, Michael Lofchie, and Jennifer Widner for sharing their views with me. I am especially indebted to Tom Callaghy and Don Rothchild for providing extensive comments on the entire manuscript.

As this book is being sent to the printer, Ghana is once again attempting a transition to civilian democracy. Inevitably, therefore, this book is Janus-faced. It is both a review of the economic recovery program that has been in place since 1983 and an analysis of the problems that a successor government will face. As a result, the book confronts many of the political and economic problems facing other African countries in transition.

Abbreviations

AAF-SAP	African Alternative Framework to Structural Adjustment Programmes for Socio-Economic Recovery and Transformation
CDR	Committees for the Defence of the Revolution
CVC	Citizens' Vetting Committees
DIC	Divestiture Implementation Committee
ECA	Economic Commission for Africa (UN)
EDI	Economic Development Institute
ERP	Economy Recovery Programme
FRELIMO	Frente de Libertação de Moçambique
GDP	gross domestic product
IMF	International Monetary Fund
KPU	Kenya People's Union
MPLA	Movimento Popular de Libertação de Angola
NBER	National Bureau of Economic Research
NIC	National Investigations Committee
NLC	National Liberation Council
NLM	National Liberation Movement
OAU	Organization of African Unity
PAMSCAD	Programme of Actions to Mitigate the Social Costs of Adjustment
PDC	People's Defence Committee
PIB	Prices and Incomes Board

PNDC   Provisional National Defence Council

SOE   state-owned enterprise

TUC   Trades Union Congress

UN   United Nations

UNDP   United Nations Development Programme

UNICEF   United Nations International Children's Emergency
              Fund

WDC   Workers' Defence Committee

CHAPTER I

The African State and the Politics of Reform

Africa is in the grips of an economic crisis that threatens to permanently impoverish the world's poorest continent. African per capita income equals only $340 compared to an average of $800 for the Third World generally; life expectancy at birth is 51 years compared to 63 years for all poor countries; and daily calorie consumption is 2,011 versus 2,468.[1] Unless current trends change, by the next century Africa will be a continent immersed in poverty and squalor with deteriorating social conditions, less food, greater energy shortages, and more unemployment.[2] Indeed, economic decline has continued for so long that the basic viability of some African countries may soon be challenged.

Africa's decline is especially poignant because it is occurring at a time when other parts of the developing world are experiencing rapid economic expansion. Taiwan and South Korea, which had per capita incomes comparable to African countries in the 1950s, have undergone unprecedented growth at the same time that countries south of the Sahara have experienced enormous declines. In the early 1990s Thailand, Malaysia, and Indonesia are also making dramatic economic strides even though these countries share many of the burdens that supposedly pre-

1. World Bank, *World Development Report 1991* (Washington, D.C.: World Bank, 1991), 205, 259.
2. Economic Commission for Africa, *ECA and Africa's Development, 1983–2008* (Addis Ababa: ECA, 1983). The study's conclusions may be optimistic because most of the analysis is based on data from the 1970s, when African countries actually did better than in the 1980s.

1

vent African countries from growing.[3] As countries worldwide race to reform their economies, other nations will no doubt begin to experience high economic growth rates. However, Africa, along with South Asia, seems to be stagnating. Indeed, while most people in the world look to the next century as a time when great advances in technology will result in a better and more enriching life, Africans have good reason to fear the future.

Given the profound economic crisis that Africa faces, attention has been focused for more than a decade on how African countries can reform their economies so that they might begin to grow again. Adjustment policies to reverse the economic decline and reform fundamental economic institutions have been championed by the World Bank, the International Monetary Fund (IMF), bilateral donors, and many Africans. As has long been recognized, these programs pose both economic and political problems for governments because the reforms require a significant redistribution of income and fundamental changes in the way the state operates. Indeed, the World Bank now argues, "underlying the litany of Africa's development problems is a crisis of governance."[4] The ability of states to implement significant changes in their economy is receiving increasing attention because, especially in Africa, inadequate government commitment has been a significant barrier to reform.[5]

Understanding the politics of economic reform in Africa is crucial when analyzing the ability of African countries to address the severe economic problems they face. But while the economic aspects of reform rest on the powerful tenets of neoclassical theory, no comparable theory guides the political dynamics of reform. The first goal of this study, then, is to provide an analytically informed view of the politics of comprehensive economic reform.

Precisely because these economic reform programs represent a fundamental threat to the way African governments conduct politics, studying the process of change also opens an important window on the actual workings of the African state. Indeed, there is arguably no better time to dissect the African state than when leaders and citizens are consciously debating how much they can afford to change the political system to achieve better economic performance. In addition, if African countries

---

3. See Steven Schlossstein, *Asia's New Little Dragons: The Dynamic Emergence of Indonesia, Thailand, and Malaysia* (Chicago: Contemporary Books, 1991).
4. World Bank, *From Crisis to Sustainable Growth* (Washington, D.C.: World Bank, 1990), 60.
5. World Bank, *Adjustment Lending: An Evaluation of Ten Years of Experience* (Washington, D.C.: World Bank, 1988), 36.

do adopt comprehensive reform programs, fundamental aspects of their political systems may change. Biersteker claims that World Bank and IMF programs to shrink the state's role in the economy

> have important political implications both for domestic relations of production (between capital and labor, as well as between foreign, local and state sectors) and ultimately for the position of countries in the international division of labor. . . . What initially began as a series of short- to medium-term measures for stabilization and economic adjustment turns out to have significant long-term implications for the choice of development strategy.[6]

Therefore, the second objective of this study is to construct a better theoretical vision of how the African state functions.

Third, this monograph seeks to contribute to the general literature in economics and politics on long-term institutional change. There is now widespread agreement that fundamental reform of institutions is necessary for sustained patterns of long-term growth. Part of this consensus has emerged from studies of the newly industrializing countries, which make clear that the shift to export-led growth was accompanied by "economic, legal, and institutional reforms that the neoclassical interpretation has generally ignored."[7] Also, economists, especially under the rubric of the "new institutional economics," and political scientists now have come to recognize that the nature of institutions has a fundamental effect on a nation's long-term economic prospects.[8] However, since so much of the basic theorizing in the "new institutionalism" stems from broad surveys of economic history or abstract analysis, a close examination of a contemporary example of institutional change may be particularly appropriate.[9] As Robert H. Bates notes, "One implication is that those studying developing areas face a subject that stands at the very frontier of the field of political economy: the problem of institutional origins."[10]

To understand the prospects for economic reform and the current

6. Thomas J. Biersteker, "Reducing the Role of the State in the Economy: A Conceptual Exploration of IMF and World Bank Prescriptions," *International Studies Quarterly* 34, no. 4 (December 1990): 488.

7. Stephan Haggard, *Pathways from the Periphery: The Politics of Growth in the Newly Industrializing Countries* (Ithaca: Cornell University Press, 1990), 15.

8. See, for instance, Douglass C. North, *Institutions, Institutional Change and Economic Performance* (New York: Cambridge University Press, 1990).

9. The phrase is from James G. March and John P. Olsen, "The New Institutionalism: Organizational Factors in Political Life," *American Political Science Review* 78, no. 1 (September 1984).

10. Robert H. Bates, "Macropolitical Economy in the Field of Development," in *Perspectives on Positive Political Economy,* ed. James E. Alt and Kenneth A. Shepsle (Cambridge: Cambridge University Press, 1990), 48.

workings of the African state, this book examines Ghana, the paradigmatic "soft" state in Africa given the comprehensiveness of its interference in the economy, and its resultant decline as it has attempted to reform fundamental economic institutions since 1983. Ghana is a good case study because, under the government of Flt. Lt. Jerry Rawlings, the reforms it has implemented go beyond simply changing relative prices. Rather, the government has begun to alter fundamental economic and political institutions in a program nothing short of revolutionary.[11] Thus, Ghana has confronted many of the crucial issues in the politics of economic reform.

As the longest sustained reformer in Africa, Ghana also plays a central role in the debate over the future of African political economies. Indeed, given the Rawlings government's success and its ability to continue to implement reforms over time, Ghana has become, as Donald Rothchild has noted, the test case for structural adjustment south of the Sahara.[12] Some other countries, such as Senegal, have not developed the political commitment to sustain reform programs, especially in the face of poor commodity prices.[13] Not surprising given the difficulty of reforms, countries such as Malawi, which did have a relatively strong political commitment to reform, have had their reform programs derailed in part by unfavorable external events.[14] Other countries, like Nigeria, have achieved temporary success in stabilizing their economies but have shown little evidence of making sustained progress on structural reforms. Therefore, how one interprets the Ghanaian case determines to a considerable degree positions on a host of complicated issues concerning the efficacy of structural adjustment, the ability of African governments to reform institutions, and the future of African economies. Thus, a nuanced appreciation of the Ghanaian experience is particularly important.

Finally, in the early 1990s, Ghana began to experience many of the

11. The use of the term in reference to Ghana's reform program is common. See, for instance, United Nations, *World Economic Survey 1989* (New York: United Nations, 1989), 174.

12. Donald Rothchild, "Ghana and Structural Adjustment: An Overview," in *Ghana: The Political Economy of Recovery*, ed. Donald Rothchild (Boulder: Lynne Rienner, 1990), 3.

13. For Senegal, see Pierre Landell-Mills and Brian Ngo, "Creating the Basis for Long-Term Growth," in *The Political Economy of Senegal under Structural Adjustment*, ed. Christopher L. Delgado and Sidi Jammeh (New York: Praeger, 1991), 48. For Zambia, see Ravi Gulhati, *Impasse in Zambia: The Economics and Politics of Reform*, Economic Development Institute (EDI) Development Policy Case Series no. 2 (Washington, D.C.: World Bank, 1989), 49–50.

14. See Ravi Gulhati, *Malawi: Promising Reforms, Bad Luck*, EDI Policy Case Series no. 3 (Washington, D.C.: World Bank, 1989), 57–61.

same political pressures for a return to democracy that are affecting other African countries. In August 1991, the government announced a program that projected a return to complete civilian rule in the last quarter of 1992. Given that Ghana has sustained a reform program for so long, this book will be able to explore the relationship between political liberalization and economic reform that is a critical question in so many African countries. Indeed, this book will argue that the Rawlings government decided to begin the transition to democracy partially in response to the problems it encountered in its attempt to reform fundamental economic institutions.

THE AFRICAN STATE AND THE POLITICS OF REFORM

There is now a widespread consensus on many aspects of the development of the African state since independence. African countries were poorly prepared for independence with exceptionally weak private sectors and with populations that had an uncertain allegiance to the newly created political authorities. These weaknesses, combined with the statist bias of the colonial structures, meant that "the tasks of expanding production, allocating and distributing resources, and building social and economic infrastructures fell, by default at times, to the state."[15] At the same time, politically insecure African leaders attempted to expand the physical limits of the state to secure their own political power. As Thomas M. Callaghy notes, "To a large extent, authoritarian forms of rule result not from high levels of power and legitimacy, but from the tenuousness of authority and the search for it."[16] The state in Africa, although obviously weak in performing any given function because of financial and administrative scarcities, continued to expand, "developing in and upon society, multiplying its specialist apparatuses, subjecting populations to its control, criss-crossing the territory it occupies and finally subjecting the activities of society to its control."[17]

A central problem of the African state has been the poor and often antagonistic relationship between government and the private sector. At independence, Kwame Nkrumah and other nationalists such as Julius

15. Donald Rothchild and Michael Foley, "The Implications of Scarcity for Governance in Africa," *International Political Science Review* 4, no. 3 (1983): 311.
16. Thomas M. Callaghy, *The State-Society Struggle: Zaire in Comparative Perspective* (New York: Columbia University Press, 1984), 32.
17. Jean-François Bayart, "Civil Society in Africa," in *Political Domination in Africa*, ed. Patrick Chabal (Cambridge: Cambridge University Press, 1986), 112. He is quoting R. Fossaert, *La Société, les états*, vol. 5 (Paris: Seuil, 1981), 146–47.

Nyerere, Kenneth Kaunda, Leopold Senghor, Jomo Kenyatta, and Ka-
muzu Banda all came to power because they controlled the strongest
party to emerge out of colonial rule. Subsequent military leaders as well
as the Afro-Marxist parties (e.g., FRELIMO in Mozambique and the
MPLA in Angola) gained power through their control of the gun. Very
few African leaders have emerged out of the private sector or because
their expertise was in economics. As a result, many African leaders have
seen the private sector, especially foreign capital, as a threat to their
political project of gaining control of the economy and their personal
prerogative of enriching themselves and their clients through the apparatus of the state. In contrast, a substantial portion of state intervention in
East Asia has been in support of the private sector, and government
bureaucracies saw promoting development as one of their primary missions. The Korean experience, for instance, is replete with examples of
government's subsidizing companies and their exports.[18]

Indeed, the expansionist and anti–private sector nature of the African
state has had an important impact on economic development. For instance, in the face of balance of payment problems, many African countries have consistently chosen to regulate imports administratively, in
large part because this type of import regime offers them more political
benefits.[19] Under a market-determined import regime, no importer can
be discriminated for or against because all face the same prices. In a
system of tariffs and quotas, however, a government is able to reward
clients by selectively allocating import licenses and applying different
levels of protection. Indeed, in impoverished African countries, allocation of an import permit is almost a license to print money because those
few who are able to bring in foreign goods will be assured of making a
large profit. As I explain in chapter 3, administrative control of the
exchange rate regime often leads to an overvalued currency and disastrous economic consequences.

Debate continues about exactly how much of Africa's poor economic
performance has been caused by these interventionist state policies because most African countries have also been buffeted by significant
decreases in commodity prices over the last few years. However, as noted
below, there is substantial agreement that certain economic practices

18. Alice Amsden, *Asia's Next Giant: South Korea and Late Industrialization* (New
York: Oxford University Press, 1989), 143.
19. On African countries' import regimes, see Ernesto May, *Exchange Controls and
Parallel Market Economies in Sub-Saharan Africa: Focus on Ghana*, World Bank Staff
Working Paper no. 711 (Washington, D.C.: World Bank, 1985), 11.

common in Africa (e.g., overvalued exchange rates, inefficient state enterprises, and policies that discriminate against agriculture) will have to be changed if African countries are to adjust their economies and begin to grow again. At the least, the policies African countries have adopted have left them much less flexible than other nations in adjusting to exogenous shocks, with the result that they eventually suffer real income losses.[20] Ghana is a particularly good case in this regard because, while it has been buffeted by the international environment, its decline was so spectacular as to leave little doubt that domestic policies and institutions had to be reformed if the country was going to advance economically. As Flt. Lt. Rawlings noted one year after his second coup, "We have created a whole lot of mess for ourselves but have failed to take responsibility."[21]

While in many cases economically disastrous, however, the policies of African countries did provide many political benefits for leaders. Often, the existing political and economic systems allowed African leaders to shift failure to the politically silent rural populations and continue to rule no matter how their economies fared. Also, whatever its economic faults, the vague African socialism that many countries adopted after independence provided rituals, icons, and a political vocabulary for governments to rally their populations around. What is striking about Africa is that in at least one way it is far too stable: governments can stay in power despite years of economic decline. Leaders such as Nyerere in Tanzania, Kaunda in Zambia, or Mobutu Sese Seko in Zaire managed to stay in power for decades despite their countries' economic decline.

CAN THE "SOFT" STATE REFORM?

Any enactment of effective economic reforms in the African states will inevitably challenge the political strategies that have evolved over the last twenty-five years. Joshua B. Forrest argues that it is not possible to predict whether or not African states will overcome the societal impediments that cause them to remain "soft."[22] Similarly, Deepak Lal argues, in an extreme example of how difficult it is to conceptualize the mutability of the "soft" state, "I have recently found it useful to think of two

20. See, for instance, Moshin S. Khan, "Developing Country Exchange Rate Policy Responses to Exogenous Shocks," *American Economic Review* 76, no. 2 (May 1986): 87.
21. Quoted in *Ghanaian Times*, 31 December 1982.
22. Joshua B. Forrest, "The Quest for State 'Hardness' in Africa," *Comparative Politics* 20, no. 4 (July 1988): 437.

polar types: the benevolent (platonic guardian) and the self-serving (predatory) state."[23] Lal recognizes that most states fall between these two ideal types but seems unable to describe gradations in the predatory state or how reversible its condition is. The inability to conceptualize the African state in a manner useful to understanding reform has had a profound effect on efforts to analyze the politics of economic reform. In a review of the literature on economic reform, Ravi Gulhati concluded

> research in political science was weakest on decision-making theory, the same area that would promise the most useful results in the analysis of the politics of reform. Political science might be better able to explain the failure to undertake reform and less able to explain why or when a country would decide to go forward.[24]

There has been little useful analysis of the ability of the African state to engage in widespread economic reform in part because few African countries have advanced to the stage of redesigning fundamental economic institutions. Most African countries that have tried to grapple with their economic problems have not moved far beyond stabilization, that is, the balancing of fiscal and current account deficits through short-term changes in prices. Thus, there have been some extremely useful studies of governments' ability to reduce the public deficit by raising prices, sometimes in the face of widespread consumer resistance.[25]

However, there have been fewer attempts to explain the success or failure of efforts to move beyond stabilization to structural adjustment. By structural adjustment, I mean changes in fundamental economic institutions that will allow the economy to grow faster in the future. Only by examining Ghana, the country in Africa that has advanced farthest in adjustment, is it really possible to understand the complete politics of economic reform. For instance, as this book stresses, strategies adopted by leaders during the stabilization phase of economic reform have profound implications for the political options open to a government once it moves clearly into the structural adjustment phase. The ramifications of stabilization strategies have not been fully appreciated, however, because few countries have moved beyond rectifying their

---

23. Deepak Lal, "Comment," in *Pioneers in Development,* 2d series, ed. Gerald M. Meier (New York: Oxford University Press, 1987), 194.

24. Ravi Gulhati, *The Political Economy of Reform in Sub-Saharan Africa,* EDI Policy Seminar no. 8 (Washington, D.C.: World Bank, 1988), 32.

25. See Henry S. Bienen and Mark Gersovitz, "Consumer Subsidy Cuts, Violence, and Political Stability," *Comparative Politics* 19, no. 1 (October 1986): 25–43, and "Economic Stabilization, Conditionality, and Political Stability," *International Organization* 39, no. 4 (Autumn 1985): 729–54.

internal and external balances. Chapters 3 (exchange rate reform) and 4 (price and wage reform) trace the reform process from stabilization through structural adjustment and are therefore able to comprehensively analyze the politics of reform.

It is equally unclear whether or not African governments will be able to cultivate new constituencies that would provide significant support for reform efforts. Much of the structural adjustment literature implicitly assumes that if there is economic progress, new groups will coalesce and support the reform effort once they see that they are benefiting. However, as E. E. Schattschneider noted in his classic study of American tariff legislation, "spontaneous political response to economic interest is far less general than is commonly supposed."[26] There may be very high transaction costs (e.g., to peasants in the rural areas) for those mobilizing to support a government that has embarked on significant reforms to help agriculture. Or governments may remain hostile for ideological or ethnic reasons to new groups (e.g., emerging businesses) that may owe their existence to the reforms. However, as Gulhati notes, "Deep-seated realignment of economic, social, and political forces will be required. The 'development coalition' . . . underpinning the existing edifice of policy, will have to be altered."[27] Thus, how African governments manage the very difficult process of constituency switching to sustain long-term reforms is a central question for this study and is the focus of chapter 5.

Finally, this book examines a number of controversial issues through the lens of the Ghanaian experience. Chapter 6 analyzes the important question of the economic role of the state in Africa. Chapter 7 examines the complexities of African countries' relationship to the world economy generally and specifically to the IMF and the World Bank. Chapter 8 analyzes one of the most important problems in the debate over economic reform: whether an alternative to structural adjustment exists for African countries. In particular, chapter 8 examines what has become one of the most controversial questions surrounding the policies advocated to halt Africa's decline: the effect of structural adjustment on the poor. The general issue of alternatives to structural adjustment and the specific question of whether there is a more effective means to reduce poverty have been discussed largely in general terms with very little

26. E. E. Schattschneider, *Politics, Pressures and the Tariff* (New York: Prentice-Hall, 1935), 286.
27. Ravi Gulhati, *The Making of Economic Policy in Africa* (Washington, D.C.: World Bank, 1990), 77.

informed case analysis. This study hopes to provide such specifics. Finally, chapter 9 suggests how the African state will have to evolve if sustained economic reform is to be possible.

ADVANCING THE CONCEPTUALIZATION OF THE AFRICAN STATE

Given that the structural adjustment phase of economic reform seeks to alter basic institutions of the state, episodes of true reform are ideal times to advance the conceptualization of the African state. This is particularly true since the state's interference in the economy, which economic reform programs try to either eliminate or make less perverse, plays a central part in most theoretical conceptions of the African state. Correspondingly, studying the nature of the African state as economic reform progresses is particularly important because demands for economic reform will inevitably have an impact on the political game in Africa.

Indeed, the policies suggested by the World Bank and the IMF threaten many aspects of the political systems that have evolved over the last thirty years in many African states. For instance, economic reform involves an entirely new way by which leaders are supposed to relate to their constituencies. Under the political systems established after independence, most African governments were able to provide a variety of resources—jobs, low prices for basic goods, preferential access to government projects— to favored constituencies. The whole point of economic reform is to eliminate or at least significantly curtail governments' ability to offer these kinds of advantages to their constituencies. As Charles Elliott has noted,

> There is a fundamental asymmetry between the way the political system [in African countries] actually operates and the way economic decisionmaking would have to operate if the demanding conditions of equilibrium— i.e., noninflationary balances on internal and external account—were to be achieved.[28]

Similarly, Richard Sandbrook has asked,

> Personal rule is a mode of government which, for all its shortcomings, is a response to the pre-eminent problem of how to rule unintegrated peasant

28. Charles Elliott, "Structural Adjustment in the Longer Run: Some Uncomfortable Questions," in *Africa's Development Challenges and the World Bank,* ed. Stephen K. Commins (Boulder: Lynne Rienner, 1988), 218.

societies. What will hold these societies together when the rulers have little in the way of patronage to distribute?[29]

In particular, severe curtailments in the state's ability to provide patronage will make leaders much less flexible in dealing with a political crisis. If economic reform policies are adopted, the state will not be able to readily offer subsidies or some other political good if a group becomes disaffected or if a leader suddenly needs to garner public support. For instance, David Fashole Luke explains that the parastatal sector in Sierra Leone expanded after the death of Prime Minister Sir Milton Margai because the new prime minister (Sir Milton's brother, Albert Margai) needed to "consolidate his political base (via the patron-client network of the Sierra Leone People's Party) by opening up new areas for the award of contracts and for appointments to positions in the new or expanded organizations."[30] This option would not have been open to the new prime minister under a long-term structural adjustment program because African countries are being pressured to reduce the absolute size of state-owned enterprises.

Similarly, economic reform will make it much more difficult for governments to buy ethnic peace by distributing patronage and resources. Some governments have established a more or less effective modus vivendi between ethnic groups by distributing resources through parastatals and rigging markets so the major groups do not feel too alienated. As Richard Sandbrook notes, African leaders will condemn tribalism but resort to "ethnic arithmetic . . . to suppress divisive tendencies."[31] Economic reform will make this kind of ethnic balancing much more difficult because the opportunities to provide patronage will be more limited. Further, when the ethnic balance is disturbed by factors outside government control (changes in population distribution, natural disasters, fluctuations in the international market), leaders in Africa will find it much more difficult to intervene in economies to restore the old ethnic order or to establish a new one favorable to them.

Therefore, economic reform, from the perspective of African leaders, creates a volatile political climate in which the threat of even minor

29. Richard Sandbrook, "The State and Economic Stagnation in Tropical Africa," *World Development* 14, no. 3 (March 1986): 330.

30. David Fashole Luke, *Labour and Parastatal Politics in Sierra Leone* (New York: University Press of America, 1984), 77.

31. Richard Sandbrook with Judith Barker, *The Politics of Africa's Economic Stagnation* (Cambridge: Cambridge University Press, 1985), 80.

disruptions must be taken seriously. The fundamental problem is that even though the urban population, the military, and ethnic groups will still be important to African politicians—because leaders must retain physical control of the cities to stay in power—those leaders will not be able to reward groups that can threaten violence, as they did in the past. Just as the particular forms of market intervention that African countries adopted made sense given the political needs and vulnerabilities of leaders, the political ramifications of structural adjustment are particularly dangerous to African leaders who cannot change the nature of their political systems in the short or medium terms.

It is true that in the long term the economic growth that the reform programs are supposed to bring about could create a friendlier political environment for reforming African governments. However, as will be stressed repeatedly throughout this book, the gains from stabilization and structural adjustment, especially in terms of increases in personal consumption, will take many years, if not decades, before they are appreciable. In addition, even in a growing economy, the reforms will prevent governments from providing special rewards for those who are politically important because of their location or their firepower. Indeed, given the way economic reform programs are designed, those who are now politically important will be among the last to benefit from the economic reforms.

Finally, on a more abstract level, state intervention in Africa has led to systems in which goods have been allocated through coercion while not allowing the market to provide information. Economic reform requires states to cede much of their coercive powers over the economy while paying much more attention to the information that real prices provide. As David E. Apter noted in his discussion of the requisites of government, "The mixture of coercion and information that a government employs has an effect on the type of system, because if the proportions are substantially altered the structural relations of government will also be altered."[32]

UNDERSTANDING THE PROCESS OF INSTITUTIONAL CHANGE

North, in the classic perspective of an economist, argues that the fundamental force driving institutional change is alteration in prices. While

32. David E. Apter, *The Politics of Modernization* (Chicago: University of Chicago Press, 1965), 240.

the relatively simplistic models of rational choice previously employed would have been content to stop there, it is obvious now that the process of institutional change is more complicated. As North notes, "Changing relative prices are filtered throughout preexisting mental constructs that shape our understanding of those price changes." However, North admits, "The exact mix of the two—price changes and ideas—is still far from clear."[33]

Applying the "new institutionalism" to the developing world is particularly difficult because so much of the modeling has been based on developed countries and the Western electoral process. Even economists who accept that politics is endogenous and who are willing to try to apply their models to the Third World often simply assume that poor countries have the same political institutions as developed nations. For instance, Magee, Brock, and Young, when trying to apply their model to developing countries, simply assume two parties, one aligned with capital and one associated with labor.[34] Given the problems in the literature, it is especially important to see what can be gleaned from the process of institutional change in Third World countries that have not replicated the Western electoral systems.

THE CASE OF GHANA

To generate conclusions concerning the politics of economic reform, the conceptualization of the African state, and the debate over institutional change, it is first necessary to analyze the actual politics of African countries. Indeed, many theories of politics have failed in Africa precisely because, while ambitious in their goals, they lacked a solid empirical foundation.[35] This is particularly true in the case of debates over economic reform where microeconomic theories and political speculation have often displaced the thorough examinations of political and economic processes that must be undertaken before theory construction can begin.

Ghana is a particularly good case for examining the politics and implications of reform. The country achieved independence in 1957 and has suffered for many years from what Naomi Chazan correctly calls a

33. North, *Institutions*, 85.
34. Stephen P. Magee, William A. Brock, and Leslie Young, *Black Hole Tariffs and Endogenous Policy Theory* (Cambridge: Cambridge University Press, 1989), 166–67.
35. See Jeffrey Herbst, *State Politics in Zimbabwe* (Berkeley: University of California Press, 1990), chap. 1.

"political recession."[36] Almost from the beginning, Ghana was a case study of all that could go wrong with an African state. To encourage clients and to enrich themselves, successive civilian and military governments continually distorted prices, exchange rates, and public enterprises. As Robert M. Price noted,

> The Ghanaian state has acted as a mechanism for the distribution of economic resources to the myriad of groups and individuals that could make effective political claims on it. . . . Whatever the original developmental goals of Ghanaian state economic intervention, economic policy has been placed at the service of political ends. Consequently, economic resources have been transformed into largesse. The securing of political incumbency, not economic development, has been the operative goal of this mode of statist economic strategy.[37]

Indeed, the Ghanaian state interfered with its economy to an extent perhaps unequaled even in Africa. For instance, the World Bank found in its 1983 study of government intervention that Ghana had the most distorted economy, and not coincidentally, one of the lowest growth rates, of the thirty-two countries it surveyed.[38]

The resulting dynamic of greater state expansion and economic crisis fed into each other so that by the early 1980s the Ghanaian state had effectively collapsed. Between 1976 and 1982, real gross domestic product per capita decreased by 3.4 percent each year, and prices increased at a yearly average of 66.8 percent.[39] Shortages of basic goods and foodstuffs became common while unemployment grew. The government was increasingly encumbered by the necessity of enforcing regulations and price controls that bore less and less relationship to reality. Indeed, as the economic crisis increased, the state was not even able to reward those groups upon whose support it depended.[40] Richard Hodder-Williams was perhaps exaggerating only slightly when he claimed that by the early 1980s, "to some extent, Ghana [was] a state only because the outside world assert[ed] that there [was] a Ghanaian state."[41]

36. Naomi Chazan, *An Anatomy of Ghanaian Politics: Managing Political Recession, 1969–1982* (Boulder: Westview, 1983).

37. Robert M. Price, "Neo-Colonialism and Ghana's Economic Decline: A Critical Assessment," *Canadian Journal of African Studies* 18, no. 1 (1984): 188.

38. World Bank, *World Development Report 1983* (Washington, D.C.: World Bank, 1983), 62.

39. Sheetal K. Chand and Reinold van Til, "Ghana: Toward Successful Stabilization and Recovery," *Finance and Development,* March 1988, 33.

40. Chazan, *Ghanaian Politics,* 338.

41. Richard Hodder-Williams, *An Introduction to the Politics of Tropical Africa* (London: George Allen & Unwin, 1984), 233.

Against this background of almost continual decline, there is a long history of Ghanaian governments claiming (correctly) that the country was bankrupt but then doing very little to change the fundamentals of the economy. For instance, the National Liberation Council, which overthrew Kwame Nkrumah in 1966, said that Ghana was "on the brink of national bankruptcy."[42] Similarly, Col. I. K. Acheampong argued that he was forced to overthrow the Busia regime in 1971 because Ghana was a "nation whose roots appeared diseased. It was a stagnated economy that had known no meaningful growth for some time, forced to live in expectation of foreign charity that had not been forthcoming."[43] Not surprisingly, Hilla Limann, who succeeded the Supreme Military Council in 1979, claimed that Ghana was "in total economic chaos."[44] Yet none of these governments took decisive economic action to reform the exchange rate or any other aspect of government policy. In fact, Maxwell Owusu argues that the cycle of coups and proclamations of a new beginning after chaos have been an ingrained part of Ghanaian political theater whose roots can be traced to precolonial practices.[45]

That the Rawlings government, after so many failures, has been able to enact some real reforms only serves to make the Ghanaian case that much more interesting. It is now increasingly being recognized that to stabilize an economy and eventually to garner new investment, getting prices "right" and even making fundamental reforms in institutions is not enough. The government must be able to signal that it is committed to implementing these reforms for a considerable period. Without credible commitment, there will be no stabilization.[46] Indeed, some reforms, notably trade liberalization, will actually make the economy worse if they are not viewed as credible.[47] Ghana's history of economic failure made it particularly difficult for the government to convince investors and entrepreneurs that it was serious about reform. Further, the fact that

42. Ghana Broadcasting Corporation, *Our Destiny in Our Hands* (Accra: Ministry of Information, 1966), 117.

43. General Kutu Acheampong, *The Fifth Milestone* (Accra: Supreme Military Council, 1977), 1.

44. Hilla Limann, *Limann Speaks: The Way Ahead* (Kumasi: People's National Party, 1980), 8.

45. Maxwell Owusu, "Custom and Coups: A Juridical Interpretation of Civil Order and Disorder in Ghana," *Journal of Modern African Studies* 24, no. 1 (March 1986): 69–99.

46. Rudiger Dornbusch, *Notes on Credibility and Stabilization*, NBER Working Paper no. 2790 (Cambridge, Mass.: National Bureau of Economic Research, December 1988), 2–3.

47. Dani Rodrik, "Credibility of Trade Reform—A Policy Maker's Guide," *The World Economy* 12, no. 1 (March 1989): 3.

Rawlings during his first year in office talked of revolution rather than orthodox economic reform made even more Ghanaians doubt that the government was truly committed to stabilization and structural adjustment when it finally announced its new economic policy in April 1983. The subsequent success of the Rawlings program makes Ghana particularly interesting.

Finally, I hope this book will follow in the tradition of a large number of analytic studies that have focused on Ghana, the first new nation in Africa, since it achieved independence.[48] All these studies used Ghana as an arena in which to discuss important issues pertaining to all of Africa, including the nature of leadership, the role of political constituencies, and the nature of the state. Examining Ghana as it tries to enact fundamental reforms will complement these previous studies, which analyzed in great detail the construction of dysfunctional state institutions. Correspondingly, this study should be able to test the propositions of these previous books, which have had a significant impact not only on the study of politics in Africa, but also across the entire Third World.

CONCLUSION

Analysis of public policy is too often separated from political science theory. It is often argued that the tools used by officials of governments and multilateral organizations are too practical or mundane for political scientists wedded to abstract concepts. Similarly, political scientists have often believed that their sometimes elegant conceptualizations will not receive a fair hearing and therefore do not try to join the debate with government officials and others concerned with everyday policies. The departure point of this book is that both these views are incorrect. Officials designing public policies desperately need political models that can accompany the elegant neoclassical conceptualizations they have imported from economics. Likewise, political scientists can use the problems and experiences of public officials to develop new approaches to the theoretical questions they have long grappled with.

48. Among others are David E. Apter, *Ghana in Transition* (Princeton: Princeton University Press, 1963); Tony Killick, *Development Economics in Action* (New York: St. Martin's Press, 1978); and Chazan, *Ghanaian Politics*.

CHAPTER 2

Ghana in Economic Crisis

Ghana began independence in much better economic condition than most African economies. It had a relatively well developed infrastructure, large amounts of foreign exchange, and a civil service generally recognized as one of the best in Africa. It is startling to note that in 1957 Ghana had the same per capita income as South Korea. However, in the twenty-five years after independence, successive governments in Ghana adopted policies that caused the average person to be significantly poorer in 1982 than he or she had been in 1957. During the same period, the Koreans quintupled their per capita income.[1] Figure 1 documents the decline of Ghana's economy in the first twenty-six years of independence.

While other African countries have also declined since independence, the Ghanaian experience stands out for the comprehensiveness with which successive governments pursued economic destruction. Although Ghana had one of the very highest per capita incomes on the continent in the early 1960s, by 1982 it was ranked twenty-first out of forty-four African countries.[2] Even though Ghana has received its share of exogenous shocks, including occasional price decreases for its major exports, domestic policy decisions are primarily responsible for its deterioration

1. Clive Crook, "Survey: The Third World," *Economist* (23 September 1989): 4.
2. Robert Szereszewski, "The Performance of the Economy, 1955–1962," in *A Study of Contemporary Ghana*, vol. 1, ed. Walter Birmingham, I. Neustadt, and E. N. Omaboe (Evanston: Northwestern University Press, 1966), 41–42; and World Bank, *African Economic and Financial Data* (Washington, D.C.: World Bank, 1989), 18.

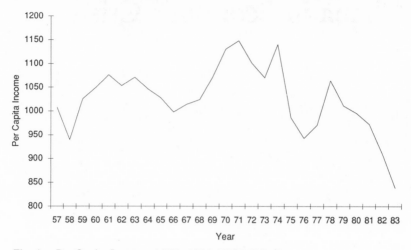

Fig. 1.   Per Capita Income, 1957–1983 (1985 U.S. $)

SOURCE: R. Summers and A. Heston, "The Penn World Table (Mark 5)," computer disk provided by authors.

vis-à-vis other African countries. Therefore, reviewing the extended Ghanaian economic tragedy is important because it demonstrates, in extremis, the processes of decline that are also at work in other African countries. In addition, understanding the economic processes at work in Ghana is important because the burden of history weighed very heavily on the second Rawlings government when it confronted Ghana's ultimate economic crisis after taking power on December 31, 1981.

THE EARLY YEARS AND ECONOMIC CRISIS

Ghana began its long period of decline soon after independence when the government began to overspend. Between 1959 and 1961, the government surpassed its capital budget by 10 percent.[3] This overspending was possible in the short run because the country was still rich in reserves inherited from the colonial regime; however, it set the pattern for fiscal mismanagement in years to come. At the rate with which government and foreign exchange reserves were being drained, by 1962–63 Ghana would have faced a crisis.

The modern economic history of Ghana began with the government's

3. Andrzej Krassowski, *Development and the Debt Trap: Economic Planning and External Borrowing in Ghana* (London: Overseas Development Institute, 1974), 42.

response to the initial foreign exchange crisis in December 1961. To resolve the foreign exchange crisis, Prime Minister Kwame Nkrumah announced that nonrestrictive import licenses would not be renewed for 1962 and that from then on all importers would be required to possess specific licenses to gain access to foreign exchange. A large number of other steps that effectively transformed Ghana from an open to a closed economy were also taken: restrictions on the external operations of banks were imposed; Ghana delinked completely from sterling and began to issue its own currency (the cedi); the government took over sterling securities held by public and private institutions and replaced them with government securities; and it granted monopoly rights to the Ghana Trading Corporation to import a large number of basic commodities.[4]

These steps were taken despite the fact that many recognized the dangers of the state's becoming too intimately involved with the economy. For instance, as early as July 1961, the minister of finance had said that import "controls are expensive in terms of man-power, and often lead to corrupt practices which we must avoid at all costs."[5] The decision to control imports administratively and to adopt the other measures was made for the same reasons that caused African leaders across the continent to avoid adjusting the exchange rate when faced with balance of payments problems. Nkrumah, for instance, had become more and more committed to heavy state involvement to promote an early transition to socialism. Administrative control of imports also appealed to many African leaders who simply wanted to increase their political power and enhance their individual wealth and security.[6]

It is also important to note that in the 1950s and 1960s the state was viewed by economists, aid donors, and multilateral organizations as a much more capable economic agent than it is perceived to be in the 1990s. During the colonial period, Ghana had extensive experience with price controls and import licensing, although not to the degree to which subsequent postcolonial governments adopted these types of regulations.[7] More generally, in the 1960s countries across the world were

4. Ibid., 59.
5. Quoted in Tony Killick, *Development Economics in Action: A Study of Economic Policies in Ghana* (New York: St. Martin's Press, 1978), 264.
6. See Henry L. Bretton, *The Rise and Fall of Kwame Nkrumah* (New York: Praeger, 1966), 65–71.
7. A. H. O. Mensah, "Some Aspects of Economic Regimentation—Ghana's Experience with Price and Import Controls," *Journal of African Studies* 13, no. 2 (Summer 1986): 69–70.

increasing the state's role in the economy. The economic orthodoxy of the time therefore coincided with the political imperatives of African leaders.

The 1961 decision to increase the state's role in the economy set the stage for a dramatic increase in the public sector's involvement in the economy. The Seven-Year Plan, adopted in 1964, declared that the state should retain control of the strategic branches of the economy, including public utilities, raw materials, and heavy industry. The state was also to participate in light and consumer goods industries in which the rates of return on capital would be high.[8] In particular, a large number of state-owned enterprises (SOEs) were established to promote socialism and enable the government to gain control of the commanding heights of the economy.[9] Often, these state enterprises and other government operations were financed by external loans (when Ghana was still credit worthy) or simply by the government's printing more money.[10] Although government investment between 1960 and 1965 was very high, it resulted in very little productive growth because so many projects (e.g., Ghana Airways, the new State House) were chosen for noneconomic reasons.[11]

Another of Nkrumah's economic policies, which was widely followed by other African countries, was taxing cocoa, the country's major export. The Cocoa Marketing Board had been established to stabilize the price cocoa farmers received. When the world cocoa price fell in the early 1960s, however, the entire price decrease was passed on to farmers. The substantial reserves that the marketing agency had built up were not used to help farmers in bad times but instead were transferred to the central government and used for recurrent and capital expenditures.[12] Cocoa farmers were also hurt because Ghana's overvalued currency kept the cedi price of cocoa artificially low. As the 1960s and 1970s progressed, these farmers turned to marketing their produce in neighboring

8. Ghana, *Seven-Year Plan for National Reconstruction and Development* (Accra: Office of the Planning Commission, 1964), xiii.
9. H. P. Nelson, "Report on the Administration and Operation of State Enterprises . . . ," reprinted in Eboe Hutchful, *The IMF and Ghana* (London: Zed Press, 1987), 146.
10. Tetteh A. Kofi and Emmanuel Hansen, "Ghana—A History of Endless Recession," in *Recession in Africa*, ed. Jerker Carlsson (Uppsala: Scandinavian Institute of African Studies, 1983), 64–65.
11. Naseem Ahmad calls this process "investment without growth." See his *Deficit Financing, Inflation and Capital Formation: The Ghanaian Experience, 1960–1965* (Munich: Weltforum Verlag, 1970), 114.
12. Robert H. Bates, *Markets and States in Tropical Africa* (Berkeley: University of California Press, 1981), 15–16.

Côte d'Ivoire, where the government paid more in hard currency for cocoa.

Continued overspending as well as increasingly obvious government improprieties caused the last two years of Nkrumah's rule to be disastrous. The overheated economy forced prices to increase by nearly 70 percent between 1963 and 1965. There were massive budget and balance of payments deficits.[13] In 1965, the government announced that reserves could not be lowered any further without threatening the stability of the cedi.[14] Therefore, it initiated a process that successive governments would repeat with numbing regularity: calling in the World Bank and the IMF. The World Bank, in an observation that would also be repeated many times, noted that the basic problem in Ghana was an overstraining of resources and that the government had to begin a period of consolidation. However, its actual recommendations were weak, especially compared to the kind of conditionality that would be a commonplace aspect of World Bank financing by the early 1980s. In particular, the bank trusted the government to enact the needed changes and simply called for financing to be available before programs were to be implemented and the necessary studies were done.[15]

Before the Nkrumah government was able to implement any kind of reform program, however, it was overthrown by the National Liberation Council (NLC) headed by Lt. Gen. Joseph Ankrah. The NLC immediately declared that it would adopt a stabilization program to try to stop the hemorrhaging of Ghana's fiscal and foreign exchange accounts. It signed an agreement with the IMF that tied its policies to certain conditions in exchange for IMF resources. It is crucial to note, however, that the NLC did not envision significant departures from the system it had inherited from Nkrumah. For instance, while the NLC stated that it would like to liberalize import and licensing controls, after it took power it announced that it was only going to reform those regulatory mechanisms so that they would operate more efficiently.[16]

The NLC succeeded in adopting a standard IMF disinflationary package of fiscal and monetary policies that went a considerable way toward reducing pressures on the economy. The projects inherited from Nkrumah that were viewed as economically sound were continued, but

13. Krassowski, *Development and the Debt Trap*, 90.
14. Parliamentary Statement by Minister of Finance, 10 September 1965, reprinted in Hutchful, *The IMF and Ghana*, 45.
15. World Bank Preliminary Report, 24 September 1965, quoted in ibid., 48–49.
16. "Proposed Letter of Intent, IMF Standby Agreement," 26 April 1966, reprinted in ibid., 64.

few new ones were adopted.[17] As in the case of state regulation of imports, however, the NLC did not fundamentally alter the involvement of state-owned enterprises in the economy. The military officers had originally displayed outright hostility toward the state enterprises, but their attitude began to change rapidly. In the end, of the forty-six industrial and commercial state enterprises established by Nkrumah, only seven were offered for sale; private participation was sought for eleven others that would continue to be owned by the state. Of the seven put up for sale, only three were of significant size. In the end, only three state enterprises were sold, and private participation was increased in only four others.[18]

Even this extremely limited sell-off of state enterprises created great controversy in Ghana and established an important legacy with which successive governments would have to cope. The NLC was attacked for even its limited efforts to sell state enterprises because many believed the government was receiving too little for its assets. At a more general level, the sale of the state enterprises, which Nkrumah had portrayed as an important way of gaining the commanding heights of the economy, struck many Ghanaians not only as an improper political step but also as a retreat from the pursuit of economic independence. The NLC came under attack because it could not provide an alternative vision to Nkrumah's on how the state could participate in the economy. The military officers had been able to overthrow Nkrumah, but they could only slow the momentum of his policies; they could not displace his ideology.

True to its word, the NLC did sponsor competitive elections, and Dr. Kofi Busia was elected prime minister in September 1969. Under Busia, much of the NLC-initiated rhetoric of turning away from the Nkrumah regime continued. There is, in fact, some evidence that economic management of programs was better. However, the government reverted to the expansionist economic policies of the Nkrumah regime. It was possible to carry out high spending policies for a short time because world cocoa prices were exceptionally high. In addition, in the early years of the Busia regime the civilians, despite their rhetoric, showed no more desire to change the fundamental relationship between the state and the market than the NLC did. Wage, price, and, of special importance, import controls were all retained. After the controversy that the NLC

17. Killick, *Development Economics*, 55.
18. Krassowski, *Development and the Debt Trap*, 118.

faced in trying to privatize a few state enterprises, there was very little energy devoted to changing the status of other parastatals.[19]

In mid-1971, after cocoa had returned to its historic price levels, the Busia regime was faced with another in Ghana's continuing series of balance of payments crises. In a fundamental break with the past, the Busia regime finally decided to address the foreign exchange shortage by a massive devaluation. This decision was a benchmark in Ghanaian economic history because it marked a fundamental departure from using state instruments as the major means of dealing with an economic crisis and instead relied on market mechanisms to balance the external account. A few days after the devaluation announcement, however, the Busia regime was overthrown by Lt. Col. I. K. Acheampong. As explained in chapter 3, the coup, coming so closely after the devaluation, had an enormous impact on later governments when they contemplated resorting to market mechanisms to address their foreign exchange shortages.

The National Redemption Council (NRC), led by Acheampong, immediately revalued the cedi, thus eliminating most of the devaluation implemented by the previous regime. Indeed, M. M. Huq is correct in noting that the Acheampong coup initiated a period of "complete mismanagement."[20] As noted in chapter 3, the decision to revalue the cedi and then to use administrative measures to control foreign exchange ad hoc led to a massive overvaluation of the cedi, crippling the economy.[21]

The NRC also kept all the other administrative controls on the economy—and added more. In addition, there was a compulsory acquisition of 55 percent shareholding in the timber, mining, and oil industries.[22] Finally, in a startling indication of just how far the regime would flaunt economic conventions, the Acheampong regime simply repudiated a substantial portion of the foreign debt it had inherited from previous regimes.

The Acheampong regime also continued the previous governments' patterns of using government largesse to build political support. As Jeffrey Haynes has noted, "Most political leaders, whether civilian or

19. Killick, *Development Economics*, 307–9, is especially persuasive on this point.
20. M. M. Huq, *The Economy of Ghana: The First 25 Years since Independence* (London: Macmillan, 1989), 16.
21. World Bank, *Sub-Saharan Africa: Progress Report on Development Prospects and Programs* (Washington, D.C.: World Bank, 1983), 8. Although unusual in degree, the overvaluation of the exchange rate that the Acheampong regime caused was similar to what many other African countries were experiencing. Between 1973 and 1981, African countries' real effective exchange rates appreciated by 44 percent.
22. Killick, *Development Economics*, 317.

military, believed that economic growth and their own political survival required the state to develop jobs, industries, and public welfare services."[23] Corruption, already endemic in the Nkrumah regime, reached almost unbelievable heights as government decisions on fundamental issues such as import permits were made largely on the basis of personal connections. While the regime did put substantial emphasis on agriculture, it was unable to meet its own goals because of the sharp deterioration in the Ghanaian economy and because of mismanagement.[24] Figure 2 documents one important indicator of the growing lack of confidence in the Ghanaian economy—the decline in the percentage of the economy devoted to investment.

Cocoa perhaps best demonstrates the dramatic decline of the Ghanaian economy. The 1970s were a time of generally high cocoa prices. Ghana's policies of overvalued exchange rates and low prices for cocoa farmers, however, caused a decline in the country's share of the international market from 29 percent in 1970 to 17 percent in 1980 (figure 3).[25] There are probably few better examples of how a nation's leaders can propel a country into bankruptcy. In July 1978, Acheampong was overthrown in a military coup; but the new leaders, many of whom had been deeply involved in the Acheampong government, continued most of his disastrous policies and did not make fundamental reforms.

On June 4, 1979, Flt. Lt. Jerry John Rawlings seized power. Rawlings said he was disturbed that the military men who had ruled Ghana for the previous decade would escape unpunished after they held long-planned civilian elections. In an extraordinary action for Ghana, a country that had largely escaped political violence, Rawlings executed Acheampong and several other military leaders for corruption. Rawlings said that he was not interested in ruling and, true to his word, in September 1979 he handed power to Hilla Limann, the democratically elected president.

It is important to briefly examine the first Rawlings government's economic policies given that his second government would embark on fundamental changes in the economy. Rawlings's diagnosis of the economy's problems in 1979, if he really had a coherent one, did not seem to

23. Jeffrey Haynes, "Ghana: Indebtedness, Recovery, and the IMF, 1977–1987," in *The African Debt Crisis*, ed. Trevor W. Parfitt and Stephen P. Riley (London: Routledge, 1989), 99.

24. Donald Rothchild, "Military Regime Performance: An Appraisal of the Ghanaian Experience, 1972–1978," *Comparative Politics* 12, no. 4 (July 1980): 470–71.

25. K. Ewusi, *Statistical Tables on the Economy of Ghana* (Legon: Institute for Statistical, Social, and Economic Research, 1986); Commodity Research Bureau, *CRB Commodity Yearbook, 1991* (New York: CRB, 1991).

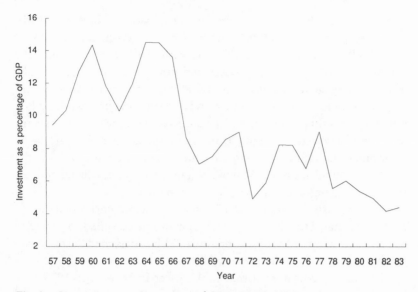

Fig. 2.   Investment as a Percentage of GDP, 1957–1983

SOURCE: R. Summers and A. Heston, "The Penn World Table (Mark 5)," computer disk provided by authors.

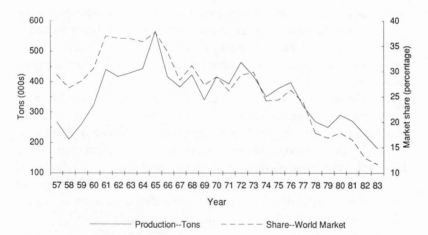

———— Production--Tons   — — — — Share--World Market

Fig. 3.   Cocoa Production, 1957–1983

SOURCES: K. Ewusi, *Statistical Tables on the Economy of Ghana* (Legon: Institute of Statistical, Social, and Economic Research, 1986); and Commodity Research Bureau, *CRB Commodity Yearbook, 1991* (New York: CRB, 1991).

differ substantially from the statements of previous leaders. He attributed "the greater part of the country's present economic and social woes" to "some businessmen who hide through the curtain to dupe the country through trade malpractices and other anti-social activities."[26] The Rawlings government's response to these perceived malpractices was to continue previous attempts to regulate the economy while adding a level of brutality to enforcement that even the Acheampong government had managed to avoid. In the most spectacular example of its determination that the state would control the market at any price, the Rawlings regime destroyed Makola Number 1 Market, which had been the center of commercial activity in Accra for fifty years.[27] The Rawlings government also declared it would conduct unannounced searches of traders and stated that if any were found with hoarded goods they would be "taken away to be shot by firing squad."[28] It proclaimed the same fate for those caught smuggling cocoa.[29]

The Limann government that took power in September 1979 may have recognized the fundamental problems of the economy, but it had neither the political will nor the analytic ability to cope with the quickly deteriorating economy. In particular, no fundamental changes were made in the relationship of the state to the economy. As inflation continued at a high rate and the exchange rate became increasingly overvalued, cocoa farmers diverted an ever larger share of their production to Côte d'Ivoire. State enterprises also continued to generate significant losses. Most businessmen found it impossible to conduct commercial operations legally and either closed down their operations or began to operate on the now ubiquitous black market. As Naomi Chazan has noted, "The Limann regime's proposals [to address economic decline] offered paliatives where more surgical structural moves were required."[30] International donors, already gravely suspicious of Ghana following Acheampong's disavowal of external debts, essentially walked away from Ghana. By 1981, Ghana was receiving only $13.3 dollars per capita in net official development assistance compared to an average of $26.3 dollars for all sub-Saharan countries excluding Nigeria.[31]

26. *Ghanaian Times,* 7 July 1979.

27. *Daily Graphic,* 20 August 1979.

28. *Ghanaian Times,* 12 June 1979.

29. Ernesto May, *Exchange Controls and Parallel Market Economies in Sub-Saharan Africa: Focus on Ghana,* World Bank Staff Working Paper no. 711 (Washington, D.C.: World Bank, 1985), 68.

30. Naomi Chaza, *An Anatomy of Ghanaian Politics: Managing Political Recession, 1969–1982* (Boulder: Westview, 1983), 313.

31. World Bank, *African Economic and Financial Data* (Washington, D.C.: World Bank, 1989), 196.

Indeed, looking at Ghana's macroeconomic indicators, there was little reason to question the proposition that Ghana had become a hopeless case. Per capita income, which had been approximately 640 cedis in 1971, had declined by the end of 1981 to approximately 460 cedis in constant (1975) terms.[32] Every organization in the country, ranging from the government to the private sector to voluntary organizations in the rural areas such as the churches, had essentially ground to a halt because of a lack of resources. It was estimated that two million Ghanaians had simply left the country because of a lack of economic opportunity.[33] Ghana had completed the transition from a prospering middle-income developing country with great hopes at independence to a nation suffering from Fourth World poverty.

THE SECOND RAWLINGS COUP

With Ghana facing these disastrous conditions, Flt. Lt. Jerry Rawlings initiated his coup on December 31, 1981, an event known throughout Ghana as Rawlings's second coming. Rawlings came to power seeking, in his own words, "nothing less than a revolution."[34] As was customary for Ghanaian leaders, Rawlings noted soon after the coup that the country had hit bottom: "For so many of the adult population of this country over the last few years, even if they have not resorted to suicide to escape the shame of their condition, there has been for them no point to this life, nothing to look forward to except a continued slaving for others to enjoy."[35] However, in the early days after the coup, Rawlings did not even hint at an economic philosophy that would reverse the plunge of the nation. Rather, in his first speech, he talked about government power, indicating a willingness to use even more force than his previous administration had: "There is no justice in this society and so long as there is not justice, I would dare say that *'let there be no peace.'*"[36]

The new Provisional National Defence Council (PNDC), as the group of civilians and army officers who ruled with Rawlings called themselves, then went about proclaiming a revolution. The economic policies they

32. Calculated from Kodwo Ewusi, *Statistical Tables on the Economy of Ghana, 1950–1985* (Legon: Institute of Statistical, Social and Economic Research, 1986).
33. Dr. Joseph Abbey, "Ghana's Experience with Structural Adjustment," mimeo, n.d., 2.
34. Radio Broadcast to the Nation, 31 December 1981, reprinted in *A Revolutionary Journey: Selected Speeches of Flt. Lt. Jerry John Rawlings*, vol. 1 (Accra: Information Services Department, n.d.), 1.
35. Radio and Television Broadcast to the Nation, 5 January 1982 in ibid., 4.
36. Radio and Television Broadcast to the Nation, 31 December 1981 in ibid., 3–4. Emphasis in the original.

implemented, however, did not differ significantly from those of previous governments. Instead, the PNDC's four-year economic program,
announced in December 1982, devoted itself to establishing a state
monopoly on export-import trade, eliminating corruption in the allocation of import licenses, and trying to reorient trade away from the
West.[37] With a flourish of populist and socialist rhetoric, the government
sought to mobilize workers, students, and the rest of the urban population to bring about (through unspecified policy measures) radical change
in the economy. Workers' Defence Committees (WDCs) and People's
Defence Committees (PDCs) were established to mobilize the population, and quite a bit of organization was done on the shop floor. While
helping urban workers, the Rawlings regime seemed to accentuate the
urban bias of previous regimes by imposing controls on the sale and
price of food, the major source of income for the 70 percent of the
population that live in the rural areas.[38]

The government also tried to coerce traders, sometimes through bla-
tant physical force, into making goods available at controlled prices. In
other words, the Rawlings regime instinctively adopted the old measures
of trying to cure the ills of the economy through expanding the state. The
regime's calls for vigilante action against anyone perceived as an enemy
of the state led to continual human rights violations by many the regime
had designated, or who had appointed themselves, to advance the "revolution." The first year of PNDC rule was replete with violent acts against
those who even appeared to be in opposition to the regime, notably the
kidnapping and brutal murder of three high court judges on June 30,
1982. As the Catholic bishops of Ghana stated,

> In the wake of the "revolution" atrocities of all sorts have been committed
> against innocent civilians by some members of the armed forces and various
> groups purporting to support the revolution. The wanton killings, senseless
> beatings, merciless molestation and general harassment continue without the
> Government showing any willingness or ability to do anything about them.[39]

Similarly, the Association of Recognised Professional Bodies noted, "The
application of the law of the jungle has resulted in the total break down of
law and order. There is no accountability. Many who hold guns or are
protected by the gun feel they can do anything and get away with it."[40]

37. *Ghanaian Times*, 31 December 1982.
38. Baffour Agyeman-Duah, "Ghana, 1982–1986: The Politics of the P.N.D.C.,"
Journal of Modern African Studies 25, no. 4 (1987): 623.
39. Catholic Bishops' Conference of Ghana, *Statement on the State of the Nation*
(Accra: Catholic Bishops' Conference, 1982), 2.
40. Quoted in *Echo* (Accra), 25 July 1982, 2.

As both the economy and civil society fell apart, it soon became apparent to the regime that it did not have the economic policies to cope with the crisis confronting Ghana. First, the Soviet Union and its Eastern European allies, which the PNDC had hoped would come to the aid of its revolution, told Ghana they had no money, suggesting that the Rawlings regime negotiate a program with the IMF. Second, soon after Rawlings took power, there was an increasing realization, among at least some members of the regime, that the socialist/populist slogans they were mouthing did not add up to a coherent economic program. Even the usually sycophantic Ghanaian press observed in April 1982 that the regime had no economic policy to speak of.[41] Finally, 1982 and 1983 were absolutely disastrous years: the country suffered from a severe drought, which caused a decrease in agricultural production, and bush fires damaged a substantial portion of the countryside. Further, Nigeria, experiencing its own problems, expelled approximately one million Ghanaians who had been working in the country illegally. Thus, almost overnight, during the worst economic crisis the country had ever faced, the government had to cope with the influx of an additional 10 percent of its population desperate to work.

THE 1983 BUDGET ANNOUNCEMENT

Finally, after fifteen months of economic failure, the Rawlings government reversed course. The April 1983 budget, announced by Finance Secretary Dr. Kwesi Botchwey, suggested a fundamental break with not only the PNDC's previous policies but also from the thrust of economic practice since independence. Dr. Botchwey said that what was required was "a complete overhaul of policy in the areas of incomes, and pricing, including the pricing of foreign exchange."[42] As discussed in chapter 3, the new budget enacted a substantial devaluation, which previous governments had deemed politically impossible. Also, as discussed in chapter 4, the new budget raised prices on a large number of basic foodstuffs, once again putting the PNDC in grave danger.

More important, Rawlings, addressing the country a few days after the budget was announced, suggested that the government was committed to changing fundamental incentives in the economy:

41. Accra Domestic Service in English, "*Graphic* Cites Absence of Revolutionary Strategy," 14 April 1982, reprinted in Joint Publication Research Service, *Sub-Saharan Africa*, 16 April 1982, T2.

42. Quoted in *People's Daily Graphic*, 25 April 1983.

> We have reached a critical stage in our history and we need to ask ourselves
> serious questions: why has it become so profitable in this country simply to
> engage in trade instead of production? Why are the most productive and
> industrious people usually the poorest? Why do we make it less profitable for
> a person to produce maize here than for him to get an import license to import
> it from abroad? Idleness and parasitism have become more rewarded in this
> economy than productive work. . . . This is the time to reverse this process.[43]

In particular, the budget promised a new relationship between the state
and the economy. Botchwey noted that "the rigid enforcement of prices
unrelated to costs of production is [not] a satisfactory basis for action"
and instead insisted that "pricing policy . . . be based on production
costs together with appropriate incentive margins."[44] As the following
chapters explore, implementing these fundamental changes posed enormous challenges for the PNDC.

Why did the PNDC suddenly change course and adopt what soon
became the most comprehensive economic reform program on the continent? The most basic explanation, and one often suggested for Ghana, is
that the PNDC had no choice given the state of the economy. In fact,
Rawlings, in his May 1983 speech, had claimed that the recently announced budget was "the only viable option open to us."[45] However, as
chapter 1 indicated, there is a long tradition of Ghanaian leaders proclaiming (correctly) that the economy had hit rock bottom and then
doing nothing to reverse the slide.

Similarly, in many other countries in Africa (Zaire is perhaps the
classic case), scholars and many others have repeatedly been proven
wrong as governments continued counterproductive economic policies
even though the experts were saying the economic situation could not get
any worse and the government in question would have to take action. In
general, there is no clear relationship between an African country's
economic condition and its willingness to undertake reform measures.[46]
In fact, as Gulhati and Nallari note in their study of Mauritius's successful stabilization effort, reform is much less likely if the country is already
experiencing an acute stabilization crisis.[47] The economy could have
become worse in Ghana and the government could have limped by,

43. J. J. Rawlings, *Ghana's Moment of Truth* (Accra: Information Services Department, 1983), 4–5.
44. *People's Daily Graphic*, 25 April 1983, 4.
45. Rawlings, *Ghana's Moment of Truth*, 2.
46. Ravi Gulhati, *The Political Economy of Reform in Sub-Saharan Africa* (Washington, D.C.: World Bank, 1988), 9.
47. Ravi Gulhati and Raj Nallari, *Successful Stabilization and Recovery in Mauritius*,
EDI Development Policy Case Series no. 5 (Washington, D.C.: World Bank, 1990), 59.

perhaps with some kind of modified reform program. Certainly, it was clear to the government that the new budget posed enormous political risks, and these fears were quickly borne out by public demonstrations against price increases in the days after they were announced. Previously, there had not been public demonstrations against the PNDC, despite the deteriorating economy. That the PNDC had no other choice is too deterministic an explanation and does not take account of the huge political and personal gamble that Rawlings and the rest of the PNDC undertook when they adopted the program. After all, given the precedent that he had set in executing Acheampong, Rawlings stood a good chance of being killed in a successful coup.

One aspect of this "no other choice" argument, however, is relevant to the Ghanaian experience. As noted in chapters 3 and 4, the economy had collapsed to such an extent that most people were paying shadow prices. For instance, given that the black-market rate of the cedi was roughly twenty times higher than the declared rate, very few goods on the shelves of stores (and nothing in the markets) were priced according to the official rate. The devaluations and lifting of price controls therefore had less effect than might have been expected—given their magnitudes in nominal terms—because people were already paying well above the official price for goods. Finally, because of the economic crisis, most urban workers were forced to take second jobs or otherwise supplement their income, so a decrease in wages or even outright loss of employment may not have been quite as significant as it appeared.[48] Thus, the extremely poor state of the economy may have made enacting a stabilization program easier than it initially appeared. This argument avoids the artificial determinism of those who argue that Rawlings had no choice but to adjust but does give due attention to the extent to which shadow prices can operate in an economy that reached the depths Ghana's had by 1982–83.

A second explanation for the timing of the adjustment decision looks to the political strength of the leader. Joan Nelson, summarizing a sophisticated series of case studies examining economic reform, argues that among the important factors determining the timing of adjustment decisions is

> a basic minimum of political support for the chief executive. Strength in a chief executive is no guarantee of quick decision, but acute weakness and

    48. Reginald H. Green, *Ghana* (Helsinki: World Institute for Development Economics Research, 1987), 23.

inability to command support from party and/or legislature or other key
support groups virtually guarantees delays or paralysis.[49]

In the case of Rawlings in 1983, however, there was little reason to
believe that he had the support needed not only to enact an adjustment
program but also to reverse the thrust of economic practice in the
country over the previous twenty-five years. Indeed, what was striking
was how narrow Rawlings's constituency was: some of the military,
university students, and some workers. All these would be alienated to
some degree if the government adopted a reform program that reversed
the urban biases of past governments. A number of coups against Rawlings had been attempted before the budget announcement, and more
would follow.

Nor did Rawlings's assembling an economic team around him (another factor Nelson cites as being crucial to the adoption of an adjustment program[50]) necessarily suggest that the government was seriously
interested in adopting a reform program. The intelligentsia that surrounded Rawlings was strongly opposed to any kind of liberalization
program or to relations with "imperialist" agencies such as the World
Bank or the IMF.[51] Further, given the exceedingly poor policies that had
been implemented since Rawlings had come to power, there was little
reason to believe that the PNDC's team had the ability to implement any
kind of coherent economic program.

The PNDC was also an unlikely proponent of reform because it was
riven with factionalism. Of the original seven members of the PNDC,
two (Brigadier Joseph Nunoo-Mensah and the Reverend Dr. Vincent
Kwabena Damuah) had resigned voluntarily by November 1982. One
(Joachim Amarte Kwei) was executed in August 1982 for his part in the
killing of the three high court judges. And two (Sergeant Daniel Aloga
Akata-Pore and Chris Bukari Atim) were forced to leave the PNDC after
an attempted coup. The other member of the original PNDC besides
Rawlings, Warrant Officer Class One Joseph Adjei Buadi, resigned from
the PNDC in December 1984.[52]

However, Rawlings and those who became his close associates once

49. Joan M. Nelson, "Conclusions," in *Economic Crisis and Policy Choice*, ed.
Joan M. Nelson (Princeton: Princeton University Press, 1990), 335.
50. Ibid.
51. Richard Jeffries, "Ghana: The Political Economy of Personal Rule," in *Contemporary West African States*, ed. Donal B. Cruise O'Brien, John Dunn, and Richard Rathbone
(Cambridge: Cambridge University Press, 1989), 75.
52. Donald I. Ray, *Ghana: Politics, Economics and Society* (Boulder: Lynne Rienner,
1986), 31–32, 34.

the economic reform program started had well-developed political skills. Rawlings had accomplished major political feats just by emerging out of two chaotic coups as the unquestioned leader. After December 31, 1981, he also defeated a number of attempts by others to gain power. In addition, there is no doubt that he had his hand on the popular pulse in Ghana as few other leaders have. Some of his associates have also proven to be politically adept, although more than a few have not. As noted in chapter 3, development of the proper political strategy by astute leaders can often substitute for the kind of intellectual and analytic cohesiveness that Nelson suggests is necessary. The technocratic input that Nelson describes is important, but to some degree, especially in Africa, it can be supplied by others (notably, the World Bank). Political strategy, however, must come from the leadership itself and is therefore arguably more important than the beliefs and cohesiveness of the senior civil service.

A crucial aspect of Rawlings's decision to adopt the reform program was the intellectual and financial bankruptcy of those who opposed it. While out of power, Rawlings had been influenced by dependency theory.[53] Once in power, however, he associated with a wide range of people, with the result that the PNDC had a particularly confused ideological view.[54] It soon became obvious, especially in light of Ghana's disastrous economic experience, that the proponents of dependency theory or other radical formulas did not have a coherent answer to Ghana's woes. Finance Secretary Botchwey, who before his appointment had been a well-known radical university lecturer, suggested some of the problems the regime encountered when actually trying to follow its radical inclinations: "The experience that we have gone through does indicate that there are very fundamental problems of social transformation that the Left is only now beginning to address."[55] Rawlings, showing his disgust for radical demands in 1983, finally turned and announced what he called an all-out war against "populist nonsense."[56]

Of equal importance to the failure of radicals to propose a coherent solution to Ghana's problems were developments on the international scene. Starting with the election of Prime Minister Margaret Thatcher in

53. James C. W. Akiakpor, "The Success and Failure of Dependency Theory: The Experience of Ghana," *International Organization* 39, no. 3 (Summer 1985): 540.
54. Chris B. Atim and Ahmed S. Gariba, "Ghana: Revolution or Counter-Revolution," *Journal of African Marxists*, no. 10 (1987): 97. Atim was an original member of the PNDC.
55. "The Right Signals," *West Africa*, 28 January 1985, 146.
56. Donald Rothchild and E. Gyimah-Boadi, "Populism in Ghana and Burkina Faso," *Current History* 88 (May 1989): 241.

the United Kingdom, many countries across the world began a fundamental reevaluation of the role of the state in the economy. The extremely high rates of growth among Asian countries had a particularly
strong effect on attitudes toward the political economy of development,
especially in other parts of the Third World, which increasing felt left
behind.

In Africa, the reevaluation of the state was marked by the World
Bank's extremely influential 1981 report, *Accelerated Development in
Sub-Saharan Africa*.[57] The report was especially important because it
went beyond the traditional diagnosis of stabilization crisis to argue that
the problems affecting Africa were tied to the way government regulated
the economy in such areas as exchange rates, prices, and the control of
agriculture. This report was, of course, especially relevant to Ghana,
which came to be seen as the paradigmatic case for much of the bank's
critique.

The World Bank and the IMF had the great advantage of being able to
base their case on an extremely powerful theoretical framework—neoclassical economics—more coherent than anything the radical proponents of change in Ghana could muster. Rawlings, notorious for his lack
of attention to economic detail, quickly mastered the logic of exchange
rate reform. The bank's message concerning the need for structural
reform was also reinforced by the actions and messages from the international community and bilateral donors. As Rawlings noted,

> Our measures must be seen as an integral part of the new wave of realism
> cutting across geographic and ideological boundaries the world over. The
> wave of realism has led to major economic policy reversals in both the West
> and the East, both in the North and the South. Both the USSR and China have
> had to review some of their fundamental economic policies. And so have
> France and the USA.[58]

The strength with which Botchwey and Rawlings in particular grasped
the bank's analysis can be seen in their 1983 budget speeches in which
both stressed that Ghana was facing much more than a stabilization
crisis. In line with the bank's rhetoric, they argued that fundamental
economic institutions had to be changed.

Proadjustment officials' ability to take advantage of such a fundamental change in the intellectual environment gave them an unquestioned
advantage over those who opposed adoption of the economic reform

57. World Bank, *Accelerated Development in Sub-Saharan Africa* (Washington, D.C.:
World Bank, 1981).
58. *People's Daily Graphic*, 5 March 1987.

program. When faced with criticism, either public or private, Ghanaian officials consistently asked what they could have done instead. While aspects of the reform program can be criticized, no one inside Ghana has devised a coherent counteragenda that could compete with the PNDC's economic reform program. The intellectual dominance of economic reform in Ghana parallels the situation throughout Africa, where details of World Bank— and IMF-sponsored programs are often criticized; seldom, however, is an alternative proposed.

In addition, the international community was willing to support its new diagnosis of Africa's ills with significant resources. The World Bank initiated lending for structural adjustment in 1980–81 to promote economic reform. In addition, in 1985 the bank created the $1 billion Special Facility for Sub-Saharan Africa. In 1987, seventeen donor countries pledged $3 billion in additional aid to debt-distressed low-income countries.[59] The International Monetary Fund also had large amounts of funds available, especially since most African countries had not availed themselves of the IMF's financing facilities in the 1960s and 1970s. In addition, the IMF authorized members to make cumulative purchases outside the special facilities of 500 percent of the members' quotas in 1981, further increasing the resources available to Africa. Finally, in 1986, the IMF created the Structural Adjustment Facility to provide debt-distressed, primarily African countries with medium-term, highly concessional aid. A year later the Extended Structural Adjustment Facility was created to provide even more generous terms for debt-distressed nations.[60] The importance of these resources should not be underestimated, especially when so many analysts are arguing that the power of ideas alone is responsible for many of today's trends toward economic liberalization and democracy. Ideas count, but the Ghanaians would not have been so fast to embrace the World Bank's views if the money had not been available.

The Rawlings regime's decision to adopt a reform program came at a fortuitous moment, just as the international community was increasing resources to Africa. Indeed, after the World Bank's highly controversial report, it needed a success story to justify its new approach and the resources Western countries were committing to economic reform in

59. Peter Nicholas, *The World Bank's Lending for Adjustment: An Interim Report*, World Bank Discussion Paper no. 34 (Washington, D.C.: World Bank, 1988), 7.

60. Jerry Wolgin, "Fresh Start in Africa: A.I.D. and Structural Adjustment in Africa," Washington, D.C., mimeo, 1990, 10; and Joshua Greene, "The External Debt Problem of Sub-Saharan Africa," *International Monetary Fund Staff Papers* 36, no. 4 (December 1989): 854–55, 860.

Africa. Ghana, a notorious basket case but with a new, committed
government, fitted the World Bank's requirement for an exemplary case.
Indeed, at the pledging conference in 1987, Ghana received $818 million
in commitments even though it had asked for only $575 million.[61] As
will be noted throughout this book, the World Bank's need for a success
story did not mean that the conditionality requirements were eased for
Ghana; in fact, many PNDC officials were bitter about the World Bank's
lack of faith in their commitment to reform in the years immediately
after 1983. Also, the IMF did not particularly need a success story, and
its conditionality programs were, as usual, quite difficult for a country
like Ghana to adopt. However, Ghana could be assured that if it made
the required reforms, large amounts of funds from international donors
would be available.

The intellectual and financial clout of the World Bank and the IMF
had a profound impact on domestic Ghanaian politics. First, the positions of those favoring stabilization and adjustment were strengthened
because they could point to the availability of real resources. Ghanaian
officials reported that a considerable portion of the initial stabilization
program they adopted had been on the shelf for some time as senior civil
servants had long ago diagnosed the major problems in the economy.
The multilateral organizations were crucial in providing support so these
officials could forcefully advocate within the government the policies
they had designed. At the same time, the fact that the Ghanaians could
argue that at least part of their reform program was locally developed
may have helped somewhat in convincing the public to swallow the
IMF's bitter medicine.

In addition, once Ghana started accepting money from the IMF and
the World Bank, radical suggestions were made untenable. As Dr. Botchwey noted, "We had to pay a political price for our external ties. . . . you
don't go to borrow money and say you are going to nationalise the
lender's local assets."[62]

Finally, World Bank and IMF officials were crucial in providing much
of the administrative and analytical resources necessary to make the
program work, especially given that the Ghanaian state had all but
collapsed.[63] As Dr. Joseph Abbey noted, "A critical element that facili-

61. Nii K. Bentsi-Enchill, "Vote of Confidence," *West Africa*, 1 June 1987, 1044.
62. Quoted in "Paying the Price," *West Africa*, 12 January 1987, 64.
63. Thomas Callaghy, "Lost Between State and Market: The Politics of Economic
Adjustment in Ghana, Zambia, and Nigeria," in *Economic Crisis and Policy Choice*, ed.
Joan M. Nelson (Princeton: Princeton University Press, 1990), 285.

tated the success of the adjustment program was the very close and fruitful, even if at times acrimonious, dialogue that was established with successive [IMF] missions."[64] As noted throughout this book, while there are many problems with the public diplomacy of the World Bank and the IMF, the provision of technical expertise was absolutely crucial to the adoption of the Ghanaian program.

The next three chapters review in depth the Ghanaian experience of stabilization and structural adjustment in two key areas—exchange rates and the prices of basic goods—and then explore the regime's ability to construct durable political constituencies in the rural areas as it continues with economic reforms.

64. J. L. S. Abbey, *On Promoting Successful Adjustment: Some Lessons from Ghana* (Washington, D.C.: Per Jacobsson Foundation, 1989), 11.

CHAPTER 3

Exchange Rate Reform

Strategy and Tactics

Devaluation is like a war. You have to have a strategy.
—*Bank of Ghana official*

Among the changes demanded by programs of comprehensive economic reform, perhaps none are more politically difficult than devaluation and altering the way the exchange rate is determined.[1] Since African economies are so open—exports plus imports routinely account for approximately 40 percent of gross national product in many countries—changes in the exchange rate will have a very broad effect.[2] Control of the exchange rate also plays an important role in providing goods to political clients in many countries, making it extremely difficult for some African leaders to enact reform. Finally, control of the exchange rate is seen by many in Africa as a crucial aspect of economic sovereignty. Thus, demands for reform of the exchange from the IMF, a common aspect of many conditionality programs, are always controversial.[3] As a result, exchange rate reform often fails in Africa. For instance, in approximately half the African countries attempting to float their currencies in the 1980s, the reform was eventually abandoned, often with a real appreciation of the currency.[4] Successful reform of the exchange rate in Ghana, therefore, is particularly interesting.

1. Interview, Accra, 21 July 1989, with Bank of Ghana official quoted above.
2. Calculated from World Bank, *Sub-Saharan Africa: From Crisis to Sustainable Growth* (Washington, D.C.: World Bank, 1989), 221, 240.
3. In one study, liberalization and reform of exchange rate regimes was a feature in more than half the programs supported by the IMF between 1980 and 1984. A similar percentage held for the African countries sampled. Fiscal Affairs Department, *Fund-Supported Programs, Fiscal Policy and Income Distribution*, IMF Occasional Paper no. 46 (Washington, D.C.: IMF, 1986), 12, 42–53.
4. S. Kimaro, *Floating Exchange Rates in Africa*, IMF Working Paper no. WP/88/47 (Washington, D.C.: IMF, 1988), 26.

In addition, the case of exchange rate reform in Ghana is especially important because the leadership self-consciously adopted a strategy designed to overcome the specific local factors impeding fundamental change. In the main, this strategy was successful. Of course, the government's correct analysis of local political factors and its subsequent design of an appropriate strategy are not the only reasons it has been able to implement economic reforms long thought to be impossible. Other factors—luck, political repression, weariness from a decade of decline—contributed to the Rawlings regime's success. However, Ghana is a good case to examine political strategy, the neglected aspect of economic reform.

THE DILEMMAS OF EXCHANGE RATE REFORM

As noted in chapter 1, in the face of balance of payment problems, African countries have consistently chosen to control imports administratively. Unfortunately, reliance on an administrative system to control imports often leads, in practice, to an overvalued exchange rate. If leaders depend on administrative controls rather than the exchange rate to ration imports, they often do not feel compelled to adjust the value of the currency to reflect differences between domestic inflation and the inflation rates of their trading partners. Indeed, in a perverse manner, use of administrative import regimes actually encourages ever-increasing overvaluation of exchange rates because the more the exchange rate becomes overvalued, the greater the benefit a government can bestow on those few who are granted access to foreign goods.

Ghana is an excellent example of how exchange rates can become distorted and how difficult it is to reform them. Ghana's history of exchange rate problems began with economic crises in the early 1970s. In response to a declining economic position, the government of Prime Minister Busia announced in December 1971 a surprise devaluation of 78 percent, thereby reducing the value of the cedi from 1.02 to the dollar to 1.82 to the dollar. The devaluation was quickly followed by the Acheampong coup, and the military government that followed revalued the cedi back up to 1.28 to the dollar in February 1972.[5]

In the ensuing years, the exchange rate was largely held steady while Ghana experienced considerable inflation, resulting in the rapid overvaluation of the cedi. In 1972, the black-market rate for the cedi was 28

5. J. Clark Leith, *Foreign Trade Regimes and Economic Development: Ghana* (New York: National Bureau of Economic Research, 1974), 152–55.

percent greater than the nominal rate. By 1976, when the cedi was nominally valued at 1.15 to the dollar, the black-market rate was at 2.9 cedis to the dollar (60 percent over the official rate). By 1982, the cedi had only fallen to 2.75 to the dollar, but the black market was at an incredible 61.6 cedis to the dollar (an overvaluation of 2,242 percent).[6]

The great overvaluation of the cedi spawned a huge and thriving black market as goods became unavailable at the quoted price. The government implicitly admitted that it had lost control of the situation by creating, in 1980, a system of special unnumbered licenses that allowed Ghanaians to import goods but did not allocate any foreign exchange for this purpose. Potential importers therefore were encouraged to bid for funds on the black market.[7]

The overvalued exchange rate also had an important effect on exporters. Prices for the country's major export, cocoa, were artificially low, and Ghana's export farmers either stopped producing or smuggled their produce across the border to Côte d'Ivoire, which was offering much higher prices, due in good part to a more realistic exchange rate. As noted in chapter 2, the overvaluation of the currency was central to Ghana's loss of market share in the 1970s. Other exporters were also hurt, with the result that the value of total exports in constant cedis in 1980 was only 52 percent of the 1970 level, while exports in 1981 were only 32 percent of what they had been eleven years before.[8]

There were several reasons why successive Ghanaian governments were unable to reform the exchange rate even though there was widespread agreement among senior civil servants and many government officials that the severe overvaluation of the cedi was seriously hurting the country. First, the system of administrative allocation of foreign exchange was extremely useful in rewarding clients because in a climate of ever greater scarcity, the allocation of an import license was a powerful means of developing and retaining constituencies.[9] Flt. Lt. Jerry Rawlings correctly noted the economic and political effect of the continued overvaluation:

> Foreign exchange is a scarce resource in Ghana and if the official banking system fails to recognize its scarcity premium, an avenue is provided for racketeers to extract rents. Providing foreign exchange at rates well below the

6. Adrian Wood, *Global Trends in Real Exchange Rates, 1960 to 1984*, World Bank Discussion Paper no. 35 (Washington, D.C.: World Bank, 1988), 122.
7. M. M. Huq, *The Economy of Ghana* (London: Macmillan, 1989), 327.
8. World Bank, *Ghana: Policies and Program for Adjustment* (Washington, D.C.: World Bank, 1984), 85.
9. See *Report of the Commission of Enquiry into Alleged Irregularities and Malpractices in Connection with the Issue of Import Licenses* (Akainyah Commission) (Accra:

actual transaction prices really means that the government is subsidising such racketeering.[10]

Many of these racketeers were either in government or had become the primary supporters of successive governments.

Second, there was a widespread belief among the urban population, the chief consumers of imported goods, that they benefited from an overvalued exchange rate and would be hurt by any kind of devaluation. One contribution to the Ghanaian debate concerning devaluation in 1982 (tellingly titled "The Revolution or the IMF") argued, "It is also important to point out that whenever there is a devaluation of the currency the ordinary people are those who suffer most from the resultant price increases, unemployment, and cuts in social services."[11]

Third, in Ghana, the concept of a "strong" currency came to appeal to many elements of the polity. In part, the need to have a "strong" cedi was tied to the desire of many Ghanaians, who had seen their once proud country decline into bankruptcy, to recapture some of the nationalistic spirit of the past by confronting international financial institutions. David Anafglatey spoke for many Ghanaians when he said,

> It is as if the IMF is some sadistic monster which becomes angry at seeing people happy. . . . One also recalls with pride how Ghana's own *Osegyefo* [Kwame Nkrumah] rejected the Fund's pressures to devalue the cedi in the early 1960's. . . . Unfortunately many of the leaders Ghana has had after Nkrumah have not had the courage of the *Osegyefo*. They spinelessly yield to the IMF pressure.[12]

For the leadership, the attachment to a "strong" cedi manifested itself in an association that developed between devaluations and coups after Acheampong overthrew Busia.[13] Dr. Joseph Abbey outlined previous governments' fears concerning the exchange rate:

Government Printer, 1964), 12; and *Report of the Commission of Enquiry into Trade Malpractices in Ghana* (Abraham Commission) (Accra: Government Printer, 1965).

10. Quoted in *People's Daily Graphic,* 8 January 1987.

11. Napoleon Abdullai, "The Revolution or the IMF," *Daily Graphic,* 7 September 1982. The *Daily Graphic* added the appellation "People's" on 31 December 1982.

12. Accra Domestic Service in English, "Commentary Rejects any Devaluation of Cedi," 2 March 1982, reprinted in Joint Publications Research Service, *Sub-Saharan Africa* (JPRS, *SSA*), 17 March 1982, 36.

13. There is, in fact, substantial evidence that the Acheampong coup was planned well beforehand and would have happened even without the devaluation. However, the political mythology that developed afterward was that the devaluation was directly responsible for the toppling of the Busia regime. See Thomas M. Callaghy, "Lost Between State and Market: The Politics of Economic Adjustment in Ghana, Zambia, and Nigeria," in *Economic Crisis and Policy Choice: The Politics of Adjustment in the Third World,* ed. Joan M. Nelson (Princeton: Princeton University Press, 1990), 272.

Procrastination of successive governments over a prolonged period in refus-
ing to adopt appropriate stabilisation policies destroyed the country's economy, given the widespread belief that a stabilisation policy, especially devaluation of the exchange rate inevitably conjured up threats of a coup in
Ghana. Consequently a succession of governments had held out until the
bitter end before attempting any sort of stabilisation policy, so that economic
conditions were particularly bad when they finally did make policy changes.[14]

There is perhaps no better example of how a disastrous economic policy
can become politically essential in the official mind of an African government.

Finally, devaluation requires a leap of faith by the national leadership.
While the deleterious effects (e.g., higher prices for imports) are guaranteed to be immediate, the beneficial effects (e.g., increased production by
exporters who receive better prices for their goods) will take some time
and are always viewed as somewhat tenuous by African leaders well
aware of the weaknesses in their country's infrastructure and private
sectors.[15] The belief of Dr. Obed Asamoah, foreign affairs secretary at
the time, that there is "realization that some adjustment has to be made
in the exchange rate of the cedi, but at the same time there is some feeling
in the country that success stories based on IMF devaluation prescriptions are hard to come by" was also a common one in Ghana.[16]

None of these factors is unique to Ghana, although that all were so
strong may have caused the country to have had an unusually poor
exchange rate policy. For instance, in many other countries, exchange
rates have long been used to benefit a segment of the population.[17]
Similarly, the fear of "IMF riots" due to devaluations or other aspects of
economic reform is a common one in Africa and elsewhere in the Third
World.[18] Finally, in Africa, general opposition to the IMF and World
Bank usually centers on the exchange rate—a widely followed indicator
in most countries—and in many African countries the exchange has
become, for better or worse, an important nationalistic symbol.[19] For

14. Dr. Joseph Abbey, "Ghana's Experience with Structural Adjustment," Accra,
mimeo, 1987(?), 4.
15. See, for instance, J. S. Addo (governor of the Central Bank), "The Justification for
Devaluation under the Economic Recovery Programme, 1983–6," speech, reprinted in
The State of the Economy, no. 2 (Accra: Information Services Department, 1986), 22.
16. *Daily Graphic*, 6 October 1982.
17. See, for instance, World Bank, *Accelerated Development in Sub-Saharan Africa*
(Washington, D.C.: World Bank, 1981), 28.
18. See Henry S. Bienen and Mark Gersovitz, "Consumer Subsidy Cuts, Violence, and
Political Stability," *Comparative Politics* 19 (1986): 25–43.
19. I discuss this development at greater length in "The International System and the
Weak State: The Politics of the Currency in West Africa, 1900–1990," mimeo.

instance, both Nigeria and Tanzania in the early 1980s resisted devaluation in good part because of the psychological and nationalistic investment that had been made in a particular rate of exchange. This aspect of African politics may seem peculiar to Westerners, who are inclined to see the exchange rate as just another aspect of economic policy, but the psychological importance in the exchange rate should not be underestimated. In a country like Ghana, where the psychology of the exchange rate becomes intertwined with leadership fears of a coup, the emotions surrounding devaluation may become a formidable barrier to reform.

THE POLITICS OF RADICAL EXCHANGE RATE REFORM

The drastic reforms in the exchange rate regime that the Rawlings government have implemented are therefore particularly important. However, it was not immediately obvious that the new government was going to make radical changes in the exchange rate regime. In 1982, the PNDC repeatedly noted that it would not devalue the cedi.[20] Instead, it simply devoted itself to making the inherited system of import licenses work better.[21] And given the PNDC's constituency—primarily workers and students—it was also unlikely to embark on radical economic reform, particularly devaluation. Here it is crucial to note that the early supporters of the PNDC were likely to be net importers, who would undoubtedly oppose any effort at exchange rate reform.

CHANGING THE PSYCHOLOGY OF DEVALUATION

Yet, as noted in chapter 2, by the end of 1982, a consensus was developing within at least part of the PNDC that the bitter medicine of the IMF, especially devaluation, would have to be taken. But both for the continuing welfare of a large part of the urban population and for government survival, government leaders and civil servants needed to break the psychology of the country that accorded such an important place to a "strong" cedi. In late 1982 the government took the first step to break the mass psychology, raising the price of imported food—until then artificially cheap because of the exchange rate—so that it was equal to the price of locally produced food. Government officials explain that this

20. See, for instance, Accra Domestic Service in English, "PNDC Member Says Cedi Will Not Be Devalued," 15 October 1982, quoted in JPRS,*SSA*, 18 October 1982, T3.
21. *Ghanaian Times*, 31 December 1982.

was done to break at least some of the psychological dependence on imported goods and to try to demonstrate to the population how the overvalued exchange rate was hurting peasant growers.[22]

The new government then moved dramatically to address the over-valued exchange rate and a host of other problems in the 1983 budget announced in April. It imposed a system of bonuses for exporters and surcharges for importers that lowered the effective value of the cedi from 2.75 to the dollar to 25 to the dollar. Petrol was initially assigned a lower surcharge, so there was effectively a different exchange rate for fuel imports.[23] Given the collapse of the statistical system in Ghana, policy-makers and IMF officials had difficulty in estimating the extent of the needed devaluation. It was hoped that this initial devaluation would at least return the economy to the competitive level it had achieved in 1978, after the last exchange rate adjustment.[24]

In general, the IMF and the World Bank oppose surcharge and bonus systems, which amount to multiple exchange rates, because they can be extremely difficult to manage and may delay the adoption of a correctly valued exchange rate. However, Ghanaian officials argued that given the political realities of the country, they could not announce an outright devaluation. The multiple exchange rate, they contended, enabled them to begin to address the exchange rate problem while suggesting to the population that they had not just simply capitulated to the IMF and adopted a devaluation. Thus, Mrs. Aanaa Enin, a PNDC member, could assure Ghanaians that "the government has not devalued the cedi but had rather readjusted it to meet the economic conditions of the times."[25]

Many civil servants argue that the multiple-tier exchange rate was also important because a substantial portion of the political leadership was against devaluation and they therefore needed to adopt a strategy that would not be called "devaluation" outright.[26] Indeed, the PNDC spent two meetings searching for the right terminology to avoid using the word "devaluation."[27] This attempt to forge common ground was a

22. Tsatsu Tsikata, "The Human Dimension of Africa's Economic Recovery and Development: Ghana's Country Experience," paper presented at the International Conference on the Human Dimension of Africa's Economic Recovery, Khartoum, 5–8 March 1988, 9.
23. Information Services Department, *Ghana: Two Years of Transformation* (London: Impads, 1983), 25–26.
24. G. G. Johnson et al., *Formulation of Exchange Rate Policies in Adjustment Programs*, IMF Occasional Paper no. 36 (Washington, D.C.: IMF, 1985), 28.
25. *People's Daily Graphic*, 20 May 1983.
26. Interview, Accra, 21 July 1989.
27. See the article by former government official Zaya Yeebo, "How the IMF Tamed a 'Leftist' Apostle," *Africa Events*, January 1985, 19.

particularly important consideration because the PNDC—a group of military and civilian officials who ranged in ideology from "Nkrumah's children" to firm believers in the IMF's basic analysis—was by no means united around reform. The multiple exchange rate system therefore gave the different factions of the PNDC a common place to meet without any group having to admit defeat.

Once the multiple-tier system had been established and it was shown that a Ghanaian government could actually implement exchange rate reform, it was easier for those who favored devaluation to make their case within the PNDC. In addition, the reform program that Ghana announced immediately drew a significant amount of support from international donors. Since 1983, aid flows have averaged US$ 530 million a year.[28] Supporters of exchange rate reform were able to demonstrate to their cabinet colleagues that the stabilization program could immediately attract resources from the outside. The World Bank and the IMF also played an important role, providing a framework for the analysis of Ghana's problems more persuasive than anything opponents of economic reform could develop.

Of course, most Ghanaians realized immediately that imports would be more expensive; and the 1983 budget, which also raised prices on a host of consumer goods, was widely denounced by the government's erstwhile constituencies. For instance, the General Transport and Chemical Workers called the budget "anti-people, a killer, callous and inhuman."[29] The Trades Union Congress (TUC) later protested Ghana's

> submission to the dictates of the IMF and the World Bank and urged it to wrestle the country's economy from the grip of these financial institutions. As a result of these IMF conditions, working people in Ghana now face unbearable living conditions which manifest themselves in poor nutrition . . . [and] high prices of goods and services.[30]

There were also widespread protests by students and other urban dwellers who were severely affected by the government's policies.

Despite the protests, the government was able to implement the system of bonuses and surcharges—in part, of course, because people knew that Rawlings was willing to use force to get his program through. As one government official said, "This government was prepared to take action. It also had a strong constituency among those who hold the gun. The population knows that if you complain, you will be silenced. If you

28. Tony Hawkins, "Star Pupil Comes of Age," *Financial Times,* 11 July 1989, 35.
29. *People's Daily Graphic,* 30 April 1983.
30. Ibid., 10 November 1984.

did misbehave you would be taken care of."[31] Or as Professor A. Adu Boahen noted in his courageous Danquah lectures, "We have not protested or staged riots not because we trust the PNDC but because we fear the PNDC! We are afraid of being detained, liquidated or dragged before the CVC [Citizens' Vetting Committees] or NIC [National Investigations Committee] or being subjected to all sorts of molestation."[32]

The willingness to use force was combined with the legitimacy Rawlings had achieved from his "housecleaning" in 1979 and the support he had gained personally. One government official explained in Accra,

> The PNDC regime had a comparative advantage in making reforms just like Nixon had a comparative advantage in going to China. It is a populist regime. People believe that Rawlings is for them. He convinced them that nothing else is possible and they believed that it must be true. A professor from Legon or a rich businessman would not have been able to get away with devaluation.[33]

Therefore, in Ghana it was not simply a question of a government prepared to use force to implement a policy; after all, other governments in Ghana had no hesitation about locking up people. Rather, the Rawlings government succeeded in part because it was able to use a particularly effective combination of coercion and legitimacy to deter outright opposition.

Further, there is some evidence that the multiple exchange rate system did work to alleviate some of the psychological disposition against devaluation. Thus, the TUC in 1988 argued that a system of bonuses and surcharges "is better than the traditional devaluation which does not discriminate in its scope and level."[34] Actually, there were very few exemptions in the system of bonuses and surcharges that the government announced in 1983, but the fact that it left the government with some opportunity to intervene in the economy seems to have been important.

The Ghanaian government may also have faced less popular opposition than it expected because, given the gross overvaluation of the cedi, few goods on the shelves of stores (and nothing in the markets) were priced according to the official rate. In retrospect, government officials are confident that more worker protest against the budget announcement and subsequent reforms did not emerge because most of the society was already paying shadow prices for the goods.[35] This point is usually

31. Interview, Accra, 26 September 1989.
32. A. Adu Boahen, *The Ghanaian Sphinx* (Accra: Ghana Academy of Arts and Sciences, 1989), 51–52.
33. Interview, Accra, 14 July 1989.
34. Trades Union Congress, "Views of the Trades Union Congress on the Economic Recovery Programme Policy Framework, 1986–1988," Accra, mimeo, 1988, 2.
35. See also Ajay Chhibber and Nemat Shafik, *Exchange Reform, Parallel Markets,*

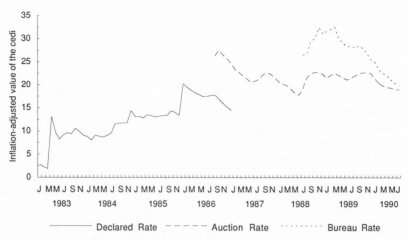

Fig. 4.   Real Value of the Cedi over Time

SOURCES: Inflation and trade figures from Statistical Service, *Quarterly Bulletin of Statistics*, various issues; and Statistical Service, *Statistical News Letter*, various issues. Nominal cedi rates derived from World Bank (unpublished data); *West Africa* (various issues); and Kodwo Ewusi, *Structural Adjustment and Stabilization Policies in Developing Countries* (Tema: Ghana Publishing Company, 1987). Inflation figures for Ghana's trading partners from Organization for Economic Cooperation and Development, *Main Economic Indicators*, various issues.

NOTE: Ghanaian inflation estimates are especially prone to error. 1985 trade weights are used for subsequent years.

ignored when government officials and multilateral organizations attempt to estimate the effects of a devaluation on the public.

The PNDC quickly moved to consolidate its exchange rate reforms by unifying the import and export rates at 30 cedis to the dollar in October 1983. Thus, in five months the cedi had undergone a nominal devaluation of 1,090 percent. The government then linked the exchange rate to an index of the difference of the inflation rate between Ghana and its major partners. Between October 1983 and January 1986, the government announced periodic devaluations of the currency, sometimes by considerably more than was called for by its own formula, so that by the beginning of 1986 one U.S. dollar was equivalent to 90 cedis.[36] According to government officials, the PNDC repeatedly "tested the waters" to see how large a devaluation it could get away with at any given time. As figure 4 demonstrates, these administrative announcements resulted in a dramatic real devaluation of the cedi.

---

and Inflation in Africa: The Case of Ghana, Policy Research and External Affairs Working Paper no. 427 (Washington, D.C.: World Bank, 1990), 54.

36. Kodwo Ewusi, *Structural Adjustment and Stabilization Policies in Developing Countries* (Tema: Ghana Publishing Corporation, 1987), 77–78.

DEFLECTING POLITICAL PRESSURE

The government carried out these devaluations at considerable political cost. The workers had become largely alienated, in good part because each newspaper that carried news of the latest devaluation also reported that petrol and other commodities were increasing in price because of the new exchange rate.[37] In a remarkable statement for a country that still suffers from what Rawlings calls "the culture of silence," A. K. Yankey, head of the TUC, said in late 1985 that "workers out of frustration would be forced by their human instinct of survival to rise up against the Government since it cannot ensure them their survival."[38] Students, too, were largely alienated from the PNDC, and the universities had to be shut for a considerable time because of student protests.

Perhaps most important, by early 1986, senior government officials were beginning to voice, in public, serious concerns about the political implications of continued exchange rate reform. In a bold challenge to government policy, Lt. Col. (ret.) J. Y. Assasie, who was at that time political counsellor for the Economic Development of the Committees for the Defence of the Revolution (as the WDCs and PDCs had been renamed), said,

> We are of the view that the burdens that tend to flow from currency adjustments fall disproportionately heavily on the deprived and poorer sections of [the] community without adequate and corresponding compensatory benefits. This sector of our society is the constituency of the Revolution which must not be unnecessarily burdened in the pursuit of growth.[39]

Similarly, one Finance Ministry official said, "Exchange rate announcements became more and more difficult with each successive announcement of devaluation. The government began to look bad. Revolutionaries asked if the government was for the workers. Every devaluation brought an increase in prices."[40] By this time, government officials admitted that they faced too much popular pressure to simply continue the practice of administrative announcements of devaluations. Government officials also expressed some unhappiness that the process of setting rates administratively, which involved the Ministry of Finance, the Bank of Ghana, and the PNDC, was too cumbersome to continue indefinitely.

37. For instance, on 5 December 1984 the *People's Daily Graphic* reported a devaluation; the accompanying story on the page concerns an announcement from the Ministry of Fuel and Power that fuel prices were increasing because of the new exchange rate.

38. *Pioneer*, 25 November 1985.

39. J. Y. Assasie, "CDRs and the National Economy," *The CDR Eagle Flies* 1, no. 1 (December 1986): 16.

40. Interview, Accra, 25 July 1989.

In addition, while the devaluation had hurt a large number of people, explicit supporters of the government's economic policy were still relatively scarce. Although farmers' incomes were increasing, cocoa production was at only 215,000 tons in 1985, an increase from 1983's level of 158,000 tons but still well below the 258,000 tons achieved in 1980.[41] Of course, the slow response by cocoa farmers was hardly surprising given that it takes five to seven years for a tree to begin to yield cocoa beans. Thus, there was no obvious manifestation of rural support for the government and, as will be discussed in chapter 5, the PNDC was still grappling with the fact that its institutional ties with the countryside were tenuous.

Faced with these problems, the government decided to institute a foreign exchange auction, which constituted a "second window" for foreign exchange allocation. As Dr. Botchwey noted, the auction tended to "depoliticise" currency adjustments because the government could plausibly deny its responsibility for further devaluations, blaming them on the market.[42] Similarly, an editorial in a local newspaper noted how the auction deflected blame from the government:

> Each and every Ghanaian, therefore, must be aware that the way he or she goes about the tasks and responsibilities of daily life will be reflected in the weekly auction results. We can no longer hide from the truth or blame it on international financial institutions or economists who talk a language which we don't understand. . . . it is our efforts which will determine the weekly economic temperature.[43]

In the first week, the value of the cedi decreased by almost 42 percent to 128 cedis to the dollar. The government soon confirmed its commitment to the auction by closing the first foreign exchange window so that the auction became the sole means of foreign exchange allocation in the country. The auction continued the gradual devaluation of the cedi: by September 1991 the exchange rate had reached 400 cedis to the dollar. Figure 4 indicates that the auction brought about a further real depreciation of the cedi even though there was substantial slippage after the auction was instituted. The same groups that had been disaffected before by the devaluation continued to be unhappy, but there is little evidence that they posed any threat to the regime.

Once the auction began, the PNDC did not comment as the cedi fell

41. Commodity Research Bureau, *CRB Commodity Yearbook, 1991* (New York: CRB, 1991), 35.
42. Quoted in Baffour Agyeman-Duah, "Ghana, 1982–6: The Politics of the P.N.D.C.," *Journal of Modern African Studies* 25, no. 4 (December 1987): 635.
43. *People's Daily Graphic*, 15 September 1986.

and did not intervene too overtly in the auction. The government could reasonably claim, therefore, that it was not directly responsible for the devaluation or the ensuing hardships. Indeed, Ghanaian authorities repeatedly noted the benefits of the cheaper cedi.[44] In contrast, the Zambian government began to worry about the value of the kwacha and intervened overtly in its auction,[45] thereby directly assuming responsibility for the devaluation and the accompanying political blame. As a result, in contrast to Ghana, the Kaunda government was forced to terminate its auction.

In February 1988, the government embarked on further liberalization of the exchange rate by allowing the establishment of foreign exchange bureaus. These bureaus, which are privately owned, are allowed to trade openly in foreign exchange with no questions asked of either Ghanaians or foreigners who want to buy or sell foreign exchange. As Figure 4 indicates, the establishment of the bureaus led to a further real depreciation of the currency from the auction rate. This further decline occurred because the auction is partially managed and because some Ghanaians are reluctant to indicate to the government how many cedis they possess. The establishment of the bureaus was an extraordinary step because it marked the abandonment of the old system, in which the government had allocated all foreign exchange, in favor of one in which the foreign exchange rate was either determined by auction, for a limited number of goods, or by a competitive free market.

According to government officials, they took this radical step because they recognized there was a flourishing market for foreign exchange outside official channels and decided they would be better off legalizing illegal trade and trying to understand the market rather than continuing to ignore a substantial part of the economy. As one official quipped in an interview, "If you can't beat them, join them."[46]

The bureaus also may serve as a lucrative new form of business for those who previously made their living exchanging money on the black market or through privileged access to government-allocated foreign exchange. Several government officials stated that at least some of the dealers who previously occupied the infamous Cow Lane (Accra's once thriving black market for foreign exchange) have now opened foreign exchange bureaus, but it is impossible to investigate this assertion. It

44. For instance, see PNDC, *The P.N.D.C. Budget Statement and Economic Policy for 1991* (Accra: PNDC, 1991), 39.
45. Roger Young and John Loxley, *Zambia: An Assessment of Zambia's Structural Adjustment Experience* (Ottawa: North-South Institute, 1990), 33.
46. Interview, Accra, 10 July 1989.

can be said that the incentive system the government has now established promotes legitimate trading activity (for which the government receives a licensing fee) and that the once vibrant black market has largely dried up.

GHANA'S REAL DEVALUATION

Ghana's devaluation is significant for several reasons. First, it was, as Figure 4 demonstrates, a massive, sustained, real devaluation of the currency. This point is important because in some countries, especially those that have adopted expansionary fiscal policies, the tendency is to let the currency appreciate so that after a few years the real value of the currency is not significantly different from what it was before the devaluation.[47] Figure 4 suggests that after large devaluations the currency tended to begin to appreciate. However, when the authorities were determining the value of the currency administratively, they were able to make large enough discrete jumps so that the slippage afterward was not significant. Each time Ghana went to a new form of foreign exchange allocation (either the auction or the foreign exchange bureaus), there was also a significant depreciation, which counteracted the tendency for the currency to appreciate.

However, Ghana's devaluation is more than just a simple change of prices. By fundamentally changing the way foreign exchange is allocated, the government has made a more radical economic change than most other countries in Africa, which attempt to reform simply by changing relative prices. The inability of the PNDC to influence the exchange rate assures exporters that they can make realistic assumptions about the exchange rate in future business plans. Had the PNDC simply devalued without changing the institutions affecting the exchange rate, it would have much less credibility; and businesses would have no assurance, especially given Ghana's past, that the exchange rate would continue. Thus, in fundamentally changing the country's economic institutions, the PNDC implemented real structural adjustment, rather than simply an adjustment in relative prices.

The Rawlings government was able to enact comprehensive exchange rate reform for several reasons. First, and perhaps most important, the economy began to grow again. Since 1983, it is generally estimated that

47. Sebastian Edwards, *Exchange Rate Misalignment in Developing Countries*, World Bank Occasional Paper no. 2, n.s. (Baltimore: Johns Hopkins University Press, 1988), 38–39.

the economy has grown at 5–6 percent a year, a spectacular performance given that most of Africa has suffered from depression for most of the 1980s.[48] Part of this increase is due to the reforms instituted under the economic recovery program, but part is also due to improvement in the weather since 1983. As Dr. Abbey noted, "We literally took advantage of the drought of 1982–83 to launch our program. It was clear to us that if we waited until after the harvest improved, it would be a lot more difficult to launch an austerity program, which we knew the country needed."[49] Also, as noted above, Ghana found that the supply of international aid was extremely elastic once the country began to institute reform. The injection of aid produced immediate, visible signs that the economy was starting to grow even when most of the Ghanaian private sector was moribund. There is no firm evidence that the lot of the average Ghanaian has actually improved dramatically, but certainly it has become evident to everyone that the economy is picking up and therefore better days may be ahead.

However, the importance of the strategy that the Rawlings regime adopted should not be underestimated. Even though the soft state had imploded, the psychology of the soft state, epitomized by the belief that devaluation would cause burdens on the urban population and prompt a coup, remained. The strategy that the Ghanaian government adopted was therefore especially important in successfully implementing the devaluation. Ghanaian officials argue that their adoption in certain periods of multiple exchange rates was crucial in demonstrating to the country that the exchange rate could be reformed. This strategy also allowed the PNDC to proceed with economic reform despite the leadership's being divided concerning the nature and pace of economic change. It seems that a sophisticated strategy on the part of the top leadership may supplant the need for the unified government that much of the economic reform literature declares is necessary. Keen political tactics are especially important in Africa because the formulation of a viable political strategy does not require particularly well developed administrative and institutional capabilities. The strategy used to implement the exchange

48. Ghana, *Towards a New Dynamism: Report Prepared by the Government of Ghana for the Fifth Meeting of the Consultative Group for Ghana* (Accra: Government of Ghana, 1989), 1; and Ghana, *Enhancing the Human Impact of the Adjustment Programme* (Accra: Government of Ghana, 1991).
49. J. L. S. Abbey, *On Promoting Successful Adjustment: Some Lessons from Ghana* (Washington, D.C.: Per Jacobsson Foundation, 1989), 33.

rate reform in Ghana took no more than a few high-ranking officials and civil servants to develop.

The PNDC also made a strong effort to try to educate people to the dangers of the previous economic policies and to demonstrate how the new program of economic reform would eventually help them. For instance, in his 1983 budget speech, Dr. Botchwey criticized the previous governments' policies of overvaluing the cedi: "The real losers in this exchange rate policy are of course the working people, the underprivileged who have no access to foreign exchange."[50]

The government further stressed its commitment to help those who had been hurt by the economic reform program by adopting the most ambitious program on the continent to alleviate the social costs of adjustment. The Programme of Actions to Mitigate the Social Costs of Adjustment (PAMSCAD) will not reverse the significant changes that devaluation has brought about, but the food-for-work and redeployment efforts are a signal to the population that the government understands the deprivations people have been forced to undergo. In its justification of PAMSCAD, the PNDC specifically noted that the program would contribute to the sustainability of the economic reform program by showing that the government cared about the harmful aspects of economic reform.[51]

There are few signs that these efforts to educate the public about the dangers of overvaluation and to show that the government cared about the population were successful in generating support for the devaluation program, but they may have dampened outright efforts to oppose the economic reform program. A Bank of Ghana official claimed, for instance, that the intensive education efforts produced a "resigned acceptance" of the devaluation program.[52]

The Rawlings devaluation was in sharp contrast to Busia's attempted devaluation, which was done without warning and without adequate planning by the government.[53] It was also dramatically different from the approach of such countries as Zambia, where the government was not fully committed to the economic reform program, little effort was

50. *People's Daily Graphic*, 25 April 1983.
51. Ghana, *Programme of Action to Mitigate the Social Costs of Adjustment* (Ghana: Government Printer, 1987), 21.
52. Interview, Accra, 26 July 1989.
53. David B. H. Denoon, *Devaluation under Pressure: India, Indonesia, and Ghana* (Cambridge: MIT Press, 1986), 166–67.

made to develop an indigenous political strategy, and few resources were devoted to educating the public on the benefits of the reform program.[54]

FAILURE TO DEVELOP SUPPORTIVE CONSTITUENCIES

Given the magnitudes of the devaluation and the extent to which the PNDC went to institutionalize the changes in the value of the currency, it is striking that more outright support has not developed for the exchange rate regime. Agriculture has improved, but for many reasons there is still little obvious political support from the countryside. First, the peasants (especially the cocoa growers) who benefited from the new exchange rates are not particularly well organized. Second, as will be noted in chapter 5, many of the peasants who benefited most from the pricing changes are Ashanti, and the Ewe-dominated government may have been unable or unwilling to become politically dependent on this group.

The business community is also ambivalent about the exchange rate reforms even though the Economic Recovery Programme (ERP) is designed to promote the private sector. However, many businesses are doing poorly because they responded to the price signals transmitted by successive Ghanaian governments and established inefficient industries behind high tariff walls. As the cedi was devalued and these tariffs were reduced, some Ghanaian businesses suddenly faced strong competition from imports. Companies in the garment, leather-processing, cosmetic, and plastic sectors have been gravely threatened by new competition from imports. The depreciation of the cedi also caused severe liquidity problems for many industries, especially those that had borrowed foreign funds under the old rate of 2.75 cedis to the dollar.[55]

Whatever the speed of liberalization, however, structural adjustment is not only about helping the private sector; it is also vitally concerned with destroying many of the old, corrupt businesses that prospered from government-induced distortions. Thus it is hardly surprising that the existing business community should be ambivalent about structural changes.

Further, the PNDC government has made little effort to develop ties with business to replace some of the constituencies lost when it embarked on radical economic change. For instance, Ghanaian business-

54. Ravi Gulhati, *Impasse in Zambia: The Economics and Politics of Reform*, EDI Development Policy Case Series no. 2 (Washington, D.C.: World Bank, 1989), 50.
55. See J. K. Richardson, "Speech by the President of the Association of Ghana Industries," Accra, mimeo, 23 February 1989, 8, 11.

men report that the government has made almost no effort to consult with them during the years of economic change. One businessman called the actual exchange rate "the business of the government," although that rate will directly affect the viability of many businesses in Ghana.[56] Similarly, members of the Chamber of Commerce complained,

> We have suggested what the actions should be, at what rate the exchange rate should be changed, but it is difficult to find an official. . . . Business is not influential. There is no consultation with government. We have government by decree. Our contribution is after measures have been taken.[57]

It may be that government leaders, aware of the weaknesses of Ghana's industry, decided that there was not enough "profit" to be earned in cultivating businessmen as a constituency. First, even after five years of recovery, industry (excluding mining and quarrying) still accounts for only 14.2 percent of total economic activity.[58] Also, business organizations suffered from the same financial and organizational problems of every other group in Ghana during the long years of decline. The Chamber of Commerce and the other sectoral organizations do not have the ability to make a persuasive case to government or the means to publicize their claims. Business therefore was hardly in a position to offer strong support to the government.

Another potential constituency for the government is new businesses that might emerge because of changes in the exchange rate. Because of the bottlenecks in the Ghanaian economy, however, relatively few exporters will be able to benefit from the new exchange rate over the short to medium term. The road, banking, and communications systems were in such disrepair that even drastic changes in the exchange rate could not prompt a quick boom of new exporters owing their prosperity to the PNDC government. According to figures supplied by the Bank of Ghana, there was no noticeable increase in the amount of foreign exchange allocated to nontraditional exporters during the first three years of the auction's operation.[59]

The remnants of the populism of 1982 and early 1983 may have deterred government leaders, even after they had adopted the ERP, from developing too close a public or private relationship with the private

56. Interview, Accra, 20 July 1989.
57. Interview, Accra, 11 July 1989.
58. Statistical Service, *Quarterly Digest of Statistics,* June 1989 (Accra: Statistical Service, 1989), 86.
59. Unpublished Bank of Ghana statistics indicate that only .18 percent of the funds allocated in the first 143 auctions went to nontraditional exports.

sector. Roger Tangri quotes a senior Ghanaian official as saying, "Government still sees wealth as something undesirable especially in a society where the mass of people are very poor."[60] For instance, the timber industry, which might be expected to be a key government constituency given its export orientation, has been under almost constant attack from the PNDC since the early 1980s because of alleged business malpractices and because it is perceived as being run by non-Ghanaians.

More generally, the PNDC did not even attempt to develop an ideological perspective based on its economic reforms. The government has not even used the rhetoric (e.g., "export or die") commonly associated with countries that have radically reformed their economies to promote exports. Rather, the PNDC tried to retain its old radicalism while implementing economic orthodoxy. While such a position may have helped the government avoid political challenges when it first introduced the reforms, it was a hindrance when the agenda changed to developing actual political support for the recovery program.

Finally, in dramatic contrast to the attention devoted to deflecting political opposition, the PNDC did not have either the interest or, apparently, the ability to design a strategy to actually cultivate support. For instance, Tangri notes that "business representation on the advisory councils and boards of government ministries and state-owned enterprises has also been virtually non-existent. Indeed, institutional mechanisms for promoting communication between domestic capital and government have either been largely absent or remained moribund."[61] The Rawlings government, not dependent on the electorate for gaining or retaining power, was uncomfortable with the prospect of actually developing real political support for the changes it had wrought. Also, even though the ERP is dedicated to helping the private sector, the government had alienated many businessmen by its heavy-handedness during the early years of the program. The tactics the PNDC used, while successful in suppressing opposition to the new reforms, may also have effectively thwarted any possibility of its developing politically helpful constituencies.

LESSONS FOR FUTURE REFORM

The primary lesson for future reformers to be gained from the Ghanaian experience in terms of strategy is that the World Bank and the IMF have

60. Roger Tangri, "The Politics of Government-Business Relations in Ghana," paper, 11.
61. Ibid., 8.

to allow countries more leeway to formulate politically viable economic reform programs. The World Bank and the IMF have developed a powerful analysis of what has gone wrong economically with African countries, but this economic analysis does not have a corresponding political logic. Instead, the bank and the fund have simply advocated adopting programs as quickly as possible. In the case of the exchange rate, they have argued for shock devaluations and moving as rapidly as possible toward a floating rate because this strategy limits speculation.

This kind of shock devaluation, however, would probably have fallen victim to the psychosis of devaluation that had such a grip on the Ghanaian polity. To make devaluation politically viable, it was important that the Ghanaians embark on the transition step of multiple exchange rates, even though the World Bank and the IMF correctly argue that this is a less than optimal strategy to promote economic growth. Thus, Ghana was a success in good part because, while the World Bank and the IMF provided the economic rationale and a substantial amount of the resources for reform, the Ghanaians themselves developed the political logic to bring about radical changes in the exchange rate. If other reform programs are to be successful, African governments must contribute a political framework.

A well-developed political strategy for economic reform does not guarantee successful adjustment. In Ghana and other African countries, too many other factors are at work to make such a simplistic association. An appreciation of the local circumstances inhibiting reform and development of an appropriate strategy, however, will allow a government to take advantage of favorable circumstances (e.g., inflows of aid, previous economic decline) to implement politically contentious reforms. At the same time, governments armed with a political strategy may be able to cope with hostile external developments and difficult local circumstances when implementing an economic reform program. The policy changes that structural adjustment demands are so difficult for African governments that the advantages a locally produced political strategy provides cannot be ignored. Even the politically adept PNDC, however, appears to have been unable to develop a strategy to cultivate long-term support. Ironically, the very tactics that the regime used to institute exchange rate reform may have made it much more difficult to garner public backing.

CHAPTER 4

Urban Dwellers and Labor under Economic Reform

The Politics of Acquiescence

One of the most contentious issues in the implementation of economic reform in Africa has been the ability of states to impose programs that noticeably discriminate against urban populations, especially labor. Indeed, the "IMF riots" that occurred in countries such as Sudan and Zambia have led some to conclude that African states are too weak to implement policies biased against urbanized labor that are inevitably part of an economic reform program. This chapter examines why the PNDC has been able to implement a series of policies that appear to be biased against labor and urban-dwellers yet has suffered almost no popular unrest. Ghana is a particularly interesting example in this regard because at least some writers had claimed that trade unions in the country were relatively politicized and that it would therefore be difficult for any government to carry out noticeably antilabor reforms. As chapter 3 did, this section will also examine how the PNDC's initial implementation of reform measures affected its long-term efforts to develop significant political support for itself and its economic policies.

LABOR POWER IN AFRICA

Observers of African workers and trade unions have long recognized the weaknesses of organized labor in Africa. In their important early article, Elliot Berg and Jeffrey Butler argued that African labor unions were not noticeably political during the terminal colonial period.[1] However,

---

1. Elliot J. Berg and Jeffrey Butler, "Trade Unions," in *Political Parties and National*

within the context of African societies, where all groups that seek to organize for political power suffer from grave organizational deficiencies, some have suggested that labor is among the more powerful political organizations. First, simply because it is somewhat concentrated, labor has the advantage over many other groups, notably the peasantry, who are dispersed over the countryside.

Second, irrespective of the amount of organization they have, workers are usually located in the cities in Africa and therefore have at least the potential to threaten the government through organized or spontaneous demonstrations. The potential for urban labor to threaten governments in the cities, especially the capital, is particularly important because in a significant number of African countries the political power of the state rests solely on its ability to control the cities. Thus, Robert Bates notes, "The contemporary histories of many of the independent African nations might credibly be recorded by focusing on major periods of strike action and worker protest."[2] Indeed, Bates argues that it is precisely because workers can exercise power through both organized and unorganized means that African governments find it particularly difficult to suppress them.

> Direct attacks on labor movements are open to reprisals; in moments of economic stress, labor movements can join with their urban constituents, paralyze cities, and create the conditions under which ambitious rivals can displace those in power. And attempts at co-optation still leave open the chance for wildcat actions; during moments of economic crisis in the cities, workers can and have acted on their own.[3]

The potential power of workers is actually greater than is suggested by their numbers because workers' actions may quickly combine with the simmering discontent found in all African cities to cause an avalanche of popular protest.[4]

Activism among workers in Ghana has been especially noticeable because, while they share all the weaknesses traditionally attributed to labor in Africa, workers have at certain moments organized to present a real threat to the government in power. St. Clair Drake and Leslie Alexander Lacy were moved, perhaps somewhat overenthusiastically, to

---

Integration in Tropical Africa, ed. James S. Coleman and Carl G. Rosberg (Berkeley: University of California Press, 1966), 348.

2. Robert H. Bates, *Markets and States in Tropical Africa* (Berkeley: University of California Press, 1981), 31.

3. Ibid., 33.

4. Richard Sandbrook, "The Political Potential of African Urban Workers," *Canadian Journal of African Studies* 11, no. 3 (1977): 425–26.

claim in the 1960s that "the main threat to national stability will no longer be tribalism, but the wildcat strike."[5] Similarly, Richard Jeffries, in his thorough study of the railway workers, noted,

> The Sekondi-Takoradi railway strikes of 1950, 1961 and 1971 were all highly political in conception. That is to say, they were consciously directed against the government rather than the management, and were expressions of protest at general policies and characteristics of the regimes in question rather than narrowly occupational grievances.[6]

Some of the railwaymen's actions, notably the strike in 1961, resulted in the mobilization of the entire community. The marketwomen and unemployed who joined the protests were motivated not only by their own financial dependence on the railwaymen, but also by the desire to add their grievances against Nkrumah's government to those of the striking workers.[7] There is little evidence that these other groups would have acted had the striking workers not provided the spark. More generally, it is claimed that Ghanaian workers may ignite social unrest because labor's own interests are not fundamentally different from those of the larger society. Thus, Kraus has noted that workers' strikes between 1968 and 1971 tended to "articulate the interests of the broadest stratum of labour, the lower-paid and minimum wage earners."[8]

Thus, many scholars believe that labor unions in Ghana can exercise at least some political power. For instance, Bill Freund observes that "a sensitive analysis of developments in a country such as Ghana also shows that the unions are conduits at times for shocks that can present difficulties for regimes."[9] Similarly, Jeff Crisp notes in his study of mineworkers that "the history of Ghana in colonial and post-colonial periods is a testament to the susceptibility of the Ghanaian state to the threat of popular unrest and protest."[10] Crisp makes clear, however, that because of a number of factors relating to internal organization and ideology, the

5. St. Clair Drake and Leslie Alexander Lacy, "Government versus the Unions: The Sekondi-Takoradi Strike, 1961," in *Politics in Africa: Seven Cases*, ed. Gwendolen M. Carter (New York: Harcourt, Brace & World, 1966), 110.

6. Richard Jeffries, *Class Power and Ideology in Ghana: The Railwaymen of Sekondi* (Cambridge: Cambridge University Press, 1978), 197.

7. Richard Jeffries, "The Labour Aristocracy? Ghana Case Study," *Review of African Political Economy*, no. 3 (May–October 1975): 68–69.

8. Jon Kraus, "Strikes and Labour Power in Ghana," *Development and Change* 10, no. 2 (April 1979): 281.

9. Bill Freund, *The African Worker* (Cambridge: Cambridge University Press, 1988), 108.

10. Jeff Crisp, *The Story of an African Working Class: Ghanaian Miners' Struggles, 1870–1980* (London: Zed Books, 1984), 183.

mineworkers have not been able to go beyond being an episodic political force in the country.[11] Nevertheless, although organized labor may not be able to be a consistent political force in the country, it may be able to mobilize significant portions of the society to protest specific policies and thereby sabotage any effort at economic reform. For instance, Jim Sliver argued that should Ghana agree to IMF suggestions and sign an economic reform program that freezes wages, the mineworkers will inevitably resist. He suggests that they will either strike, depleting the country's foreign exchange reserves, or rebel while staying on the job, severely reducing the country's flow of minerals.[12]

ECONOMIC REFORM AND LABOR

Precisely because they are able to exercise at least some political power, workers, especially in the urban areas, have been able to receive a disproportionate share of the political goods distributed by African governments across the continent. A central theme in Bates's book is that fear of unrest on the part of urban workers has been a consistent factor in the drive by African governments to keep food prices as low as possible. Thus, to buy the political acquiescence of workers and city-dwellers, governments have taxed the peasants. In addition, many African governments have found it politically convenient to try to co-opt the urban population by padding state-owned enterprises with as many surplus workers as possible. Also, the urban population has traditionally benefited from subsidies on fuel and government services not usually available to the rural population. Finally, the urban population has often been the beneficiary of artificially cheap imported goods, especially food but also clothes and other consumer goods, brought into the country when the currency has been overvalued.

Not surprisingly, therefore, urban workers are one of the chief targets of economic reform programs that hope to bring about fundamental changes in African economies. As noted in chapter 3, most economic reform programs hope to devalue the local currency and thereby increase the price of many goods consumed primarily by the urban population. These economic reform programs also seek to reduce government spending and subsidies on crucial commodities such as food, fuel, and trans-

11. Ibid., 183–84.
12. Jim Sliver, "Class Struggles in Ghana's Mining Industry," *Review of African Political Economy,* no. 12 (May–August 1978): 86.

port that the urban population benefits from disproportionately.[13] Finally, many reform programs demand sharp reductions in the staffing of public-sector enterprises; such reductions inevitably increase unemployment among the urban working class.

In the short run, the urban population is almost certain to face nothing but relative income losses; thus, labor will be tempted to mobilize to block economic reform programs. The fact that so much of the cost of economic reform will be visible immediately plays to the urban working class's political strength. The potential for strikes and labor unrest igniting more general popular protest will clearly be greatest during a drastic program that suddenly causes a sharp deterioration in the standard of urban living. Thus, especially in the first few years of any economic reform program, one of the central questions for any government is whether it can contain labor protests until the benefits of the reforms become obvious to workers.

In Ghana, much of the reform program was ostensibly directed against the urban population. For instance, the devaluation of the cedi, discussed in chapter 3, had a disproportionate effect on the urban population, which consumed most of the imported goods. Also, beginning in the 1983 budget, the government embarked on a radical reform of prices. Subsidies for many government services were eliminated with the result that the urban population was faced with sudden price increases for basic goods: hospital fees were introduced in 1983 and increased in 1985; water fees rose 150 percent; postal tariffs increased 365 percent; and electricity rates rose 1,000 percent.[14] There was also a dramatic effort to reform price controls. Previous governments had established a byzantine system of regulating close to 6,000 prices on nearly 700 producer groups. The PNDC quickly abolished almost all these controls. By the late 1980s, only a handful of price controls still existed, and these regulations had only a minimal effect on the pricing decisions of companies.[15] Indeed, Rawlings went out of his way to emphasize that the removal of price controls was an antiurban move. For instance, in his first speech after the Economic Recovery Programme (ERP) was

13. Of the forty-one IMF programs in sub-Saharan Africa between 1980 and 1986, 85 percent put limits on government borrowing and expenditures and almost 90 percent demanded a reduction in the fiscal deficit. William Jaeger and Charles Humphreys, "The Effect of Policy Reforms on Agricultural Incentives in Sub-Saharan Africa," *American Journal of Agricultural Economics* 70, no. 5 (December 1988): 1037.

14. N. Bentsi-Enchill, "Paying the Price," *West Africa*, 13 January 1986, 78.

15. World Bank Staff, "Removing Price Controls in Ghana," in *Industrial Adjustment in Sub-Saharan Africa*, ed. Gerald M. Meier and William F. Steel (New York: Oxford University Press, 1989), 180–82.

announced, Rawlings defended the kerosene price increases in part because the majority of the fuel was not marketed in the rural areas.[16]

Since 1983, the government of Ghana has also embarked on a wide-ranging program to reform state-owned enterprises that has as its central mission the reduction of surplus workers. For instance, in the mid-1980s, the government undertook an evaluation and redeployment exercise that reduced the size of the Cocoa Board's payroll from 100,000 employees to 50,000. Other state enterprises are undergoing similar programs, although none can claim quite the extravagance of waste that the Cocoa Board achieved. The government is also hoping to reduce its own work force, and the ERP includes plans to eliminate approximately 36,000 positions from a total civil service of approximately 540,000.

Finally, the government has made it clear through its intervention in the wage process that it is not going to allow significant wage increases for workers in the near future for fear of reigniting inflation. Rawlings warned the Trades Union Congress when it was reformulated in December 1983 that "many members of the general public see the TUC as an organisation which has attempted in the past to hold the rest of the community to ransom."[17] Also, the government has declared that it is not in the business of promoting the wages of workers. Although Ghana has retained its Prices and Incomes Board (PIB), this body now only regulates wages. In 1988, for instance, when some companies agreed to raise the incomes of their workers by 30 to 50 percent, the PIB decreed that no raises of greater than 25 percent would be allowed.[18] In addition, if employers promise workers a wage increase but have not paid their taxes and social security contributions and put aside money for terminal benefits, the board will make them reduce the size of the wage increase to meet these other commitments.[19] Ghana still sets a minimum wage, but the Employers Association of Ghana reports that the wage is so low that most employers, especially in the major urban areas, are already paying it. In addition, the government does not have the ability to monitor those employers in the rural areas who do not pay the minimum wage.[20]

Thus, workers in Ghana, at least some of whom have been portrayed

16. J. J. Rawlings, *Ghana's Moment of Truth* (Accra: Information Services Department, 1983), 8.

17. J. J. Rawlings, "Address to the Plenary Session of the Third Quadrennial Congress of the TUC," reprinted in *Forging Ahead: Selected Speeches of Flt. Lt. Jerry John Rawlings,* vol. 2 (Accra: Information Services Department, 1983), 56.

18. H. T. Mbiah, "Towards a National Wages Policy in Ghana," 10 October 1989, Tema, mimeo, 3.

19. Interview, Accra, 26 September 1989.

20. Interview, Accra, 31 July 1989.

as having a history of antistate activity, have been hit by what appears to be a large number of blows over the last few years. As the Trades Union Congress noted,

> Although the various statistical indicators are moving in the desired directions under the nation's Economic Recovery Programme, the going is still hard for the working people. . . . The sum effect of the IMF and World Bank sponsored economic policies are the cheapening of the local currency through the foreign exchange auction system, the high rates of unemployment and a rising cost of living brought about by the decontrolling of prices, removal of subsidies on essential goods and services and the partial freeze on wages and salaries of the working people.[21]

Certainly, the ERP has instituted more far-reaching changes in the economy than either the 1961 or 1971 budgets, which sparked much worker unrest. Indeed, the Ghanaian reforms are near the magnitude of the Zambian price increases that caused large-scale rioting and the eventual abandonment of that reform program in 1986.

However, since the massive reform program was first announced in 1983, Ghana has not experienced significant popular unrest ignited by organized or unorganized labor (or anyone else for that matter). As figure 5 shows, while there have been some strikes, labor unrest is not as high as it was in the 1970s; indeed, currently there are fewer strikes in Ghana than there have ever been. Despite the government's economic policies, protests have been few.

Why has labor acquiesced to these economic reforms, especially given Ghana's history? The explanation given by many Ghanaians, within both government and the Trades Union Congress, derives from a belief that Ghanaians desire to avoid conflict and that they will stand for almost any government action. As one Ministry of Finance official noted in an interview, "The Ghanaian has his own personality. If this would have been Nigeria, heads would have rolled."[22] This explanation is particularly unsatisfactory, however, given that Ghana has had, if anything, a more active labor movement than most other African countries over the last twenty-five years. Certainly, very few, if any, of the authors who studied Ghanaian labor movements in the 1960s and 1970s pictured Ghanaian workers as particularly acquiescent, and the mobilization of workers during 1982 makes this argument particularly unpersuasive.

21. Trades Union Congress, "Economic Survey of Ghana, 1980–1987," Accra, mimeo, 1988, 32.
22. Interview, Accra, 19 July 1989.

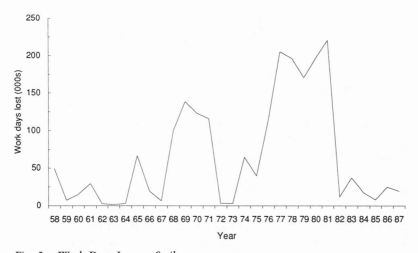

Fig. 5. Work Days Lost to Strikes

SOURCE: International Labour Organization, *Yearbook of Labour Statistics* (Geneva: International Labour Organization, various years).

EXPLAINING POLITICAL ACQUIESCENCE

Despite the PNDC's previous efforts at mobilizing the workers, the devaluation and increases in prices that the government announced in April 1983, as well as the firm indication that more costly reforms were on the way, led to immediate union protests. As noted in chapter 3, the unions were exceptionally vocal in their protests. Many workers went beyond these statements and publicly protested the budget. For instance, worker protests prevented a speech by Finance Secretary Kwesi Botchwey in Kumasi in May 1983.[23]

In the crucial period immediately after the budget announcement, however, the government was able to survive with little difficulty. Workers blustered, but did not take to the streets. Similarly, as figure 5 indicates, although there was an upsurge in strikes in 1983, it was not a significant increase compared to previous labor activism in Ghana. Indeed, there are some indications that in the period immediately after the budget announcement, the PNDC retained the support of at least some of the workers. For instance, Hansen notes that when the regime faced its most severe coup threat on June 19, 1983, the WDCs mounted road blocks and rallied to support the regime.[24]

23. *People's Daily Graphic*, 13 May 1983.
24. Emmanuel Hansen, "The State and Popular Struggles in Ghana, 1982–1986," in

There are probably several reasons why workers did not organize in
the days immediately after the coup and present a significant challenge to
the government. The first factor, usually ignored in political studies, is
simply chance. Large mob actions of the type that African governments
fear most usually form spontaneously, and it may just have been that the
mob did not come together in the right manner. Once a few days had
elapsed, the moment for mass popular protest had passed.

Second, the PNDC had destroyed much of the unions' traditional
leadership and replaced it with people who owed their political survival
to Rawlings. The new regime viewed the existing trade union leadership
as part of the problem to be overcome rather than part of the solution. As
Rawlings noted in a speech in 1987, "The traditional union movement,
like other institutions . . . has had its own history of power being ex-
ercised by a few who do not always express the real interests of that
constituency."[25] Beginning shortly after the December 31 coup, the previously elected TUC officials were subject to continual harassment. For
instance, in January 1982, sixteen general secretaries of various unions
were "reported to have gone into hiding for fear of molestation by the
workers, some of whom cursed and cried for their blood."[26] In April
1982, the existing union leadership was deposed, and the TUC was
placed under the control of an appointed Interim Management Committee made up of radical supporters of the new regime.[27]

The Workers' Defence Committees, especially as they operated during
1982, can also be seen as a profound challenge to the organized union
structures that were supposed to represent workers' interests on the shop
floor. Certainly, other Ghanaian governments had attempted to co-opt
the labor movement. However, this was the first time in the nation's
history that a regime had gone so far as to try to supplant actual union
organization on the shop floor. As Emmanuel Hansen noted, "The
WDC's became the main centres for the expression of shop-floor mili-
tancy and struggle within the labour process, first for the control of the
labour movement and secondly for the control of the labour process
itself."[28]

The PNDC was therefore able to mobilize a significant number of

Popular Struggles for Democracy in Africa, ed. Peter Anyang' Nyong'o (London: Zed
Books, 1987), 181.
   25. *People's Daily Graphic,* 8 January 1987.
   26. *Echo,* 31 January 1982.
   27. U.S. Department of Labor, *Foreign Labor Trends: Ghana* (Washington, D.C.: U.S.
Department of Labor, 1989), 4.
   28. Hansen, "Popular Struggles," 179.

workers, although outside normal union channels. For instance, when the Ghana Textile Products Company in February 1982 threatened to lay off half its workers because of the country's grave economic condition, the workers took over the factory. The government did nothing until March 1983, when the police attacked a WDC march in Tema. It then intervened and supported the workers, condemned the police action, and deported the expatriate manager.[29] More generally, workers turned out in large numbers at the continual rallies the PNDC had during 1982.

The new labor leaders, who had been appointed outside the traditional labor union structure, were then fatally compromised when the PNDC announced its economic reform package in 1983. There was no denying that the PNDC had made a fundamental reversal in its economic policies and that labor was no longer seen as particularly important to the regime. But no core of leaders existed around whom workers could coalesce in a concentrated wave of antiregime protests. In fact, the only leaders the workers had "appealed to workers to exercise utmost restraint whilst the leaders engage in consultation with the government in order not to jeopardize the long-term goals of the workers' struggles."[30]

Third, as with the devaluation, much of the urban population was already paying higher prices through the black market. Indeed, as early as 1970, Tony Killick had found that only 17 percent of items in stores were priced according to government controls; 11 percent were below the control price, but 72 percent of the goods actually cost more than they should have. In the urban areas, where most of the workers were concentrated, there was only a 30 percent observance rate.[31] Given the decay that Ghanaian administrative structures underwent after 1970, it is likely that even fewer of the controlled prices were being observed by the early 1980s. As one Ministry of Finance official noted,

> It was not too difficult to reduce price controls. Price controls were for civil servants and others whose salaries were high . . . the only merchandise that was available was from the black market. You were lucky to get one bar of soap at the controlled price.[32]

29. S. K. Kwakyi, "A Study of Social and Political Struggles in Ghana since 31st December 1981: A Case Study of TUC/Government Relations," Honors Thesis, Department of Political Science, University of Ghana, Legon, 1988, 30.

30. *People's Daily Graphic*, 25 April 1983.

31. Tony Killick, *Development Economics in Action: A Study of Economic Policies in Ghana* (New York: St. Martin's Press, 1978), 288.

32. Interview, Accra, 25 July 1990.

In fact, the black market prices that most urban dwellers paid were, as explained in chapter 3, probably at least as high as shadow prices for most basic commodities.

Finally, the role of government repression must be made clear. Rawlings earned a universal reputation for being tough after he ordered the execution of three former heads of state. This reputation was bolstered by severe human rights violations during the first year of the PNDC. It must have been easy for the workers to imagine that the regime was more than willing to turn its violence on them should they publicly oppose the new reforms. Indeed, Finance Secretary Botchwey immediately made clear that criticism of the budget would be seen as a disloyal act:

> The sudden alliance between certain negative elements in society and workers following the release of the 1983 budget is an attempt by such elements to hide behind legitimate workers' grievances and subvert an economic programme meant to put the economy right.[33]

Similarly, in 1988, shortly before the TUC was to elect a new leadership, Kojo Tsikata, the PNDC member in charge of security, warned,

> The trade union movement is like a ship. . . . If we permit these infantile leftists, these super revolutionaries, these people who want to be more Catholic than the Pope to seize control of this ship . . . well for those of you who can swim "good luck," but for those of you who cannot swim, you better say your last prayers.[34]

Bates and others have noted that repression against trade unions often does not work because, especially in Africa, threats to the government usually come in the form of wildcat strikes rather than organized actions, which can be prevented by locking up leaders. However, the particular type of repression so evident in 1982, when violence was directed in a highly decentralized manner against many members of society, may have inadvertently deterred workers from engaging in any kind of antiregime activity because it was clear that even the ordinary person was susceptible to repression. Of course, the central role that repression played suggests that arguments about the political nature of Ghanaians have relatively little relevance in understanding the unfolding of post-1983 developments.

In fact, government repression did have a significant effect on labor's calculations concerning the amount of political space it had to operate

33. *People's Daily Graphic,* 27 April 1983.
34. Quoted by K. Owusu, "Caring and Sharing?" *West Africa,* 23 July 1990, 2152.

in. In December 1983, the interim committee of the TUC was voted out, and many pretakeover leaders of the congress were returned to power. The new leadership continued to attack the evolving economic reform program of the government. A. K. Yankey, the new head of the TUC, said, "The plain truth is that the ordinary Ghanaian, the poor worker, is suffering. And the government must know that there is a limit to human endurance."[35] Similarly, a resolution adopted by the TUC executive board in 1984 noted that

> as a result of these IMF and World Bank conditions, the working people of Ghana now face unbearable conditions of life expressed in poor nutrition, high prices of goods and services, inadequate housing, continuing deterioration of social services and growing unemployment above all. . . . We caution government that the above conditions pose serious implications for the sharpening of class conflict in the society.[36]

In addition, sporadic worker protests embarrassed the regime. For instance, in January 1986, after a minimum wage announcement, workers in Tema marched through the streets while the local labor coordinator said that the increase in the minimum wage represented nothing more than "a slave-wage which is not our choice."[37]

However, while they continued to agitate about the reforms, union leaders clearly recognized that, given the nature and history of the PNDC, there were real limits to the government's patience in confronting actual protests. For instance, when the TUC sought to protest the Cocoa Board's retrenchments and the matter of paying out terminal benefits, the PNDC surrounded the TUC headquarters with armored cars.[38] Accordingly, trade union officials have adjusted their tactics. As one senior TUC official told me,

> The TUC knows that if it had a militant policy with strikes it might end with the dissolution of the TUC. Then we would have the double task of trying to get reinstated and to help protect the workers' movement. We are working toward the survival of the workers' movement. Therefore, we use these methods [talks with government] rather than violence.[39]

In addition, the TUC was also handicapped by not having the analytic and organizational ability to develop an alternative to the government's

35. *Pioneer,* 21 September 1984.
36. Ibid., 5 November 1984.
37. Ibid., 22 January 1986.
38. "Paying the Price," *West Africa,* 13 January 1986, 78.
39. Interview, Accra, 27 September 1989.

programs. The labor movement's organizational ability had been greatly weakened by the long economic decline and the various changes in leadership that the PNDC had engineered. Thus, protests against the government could only be viewed as a negative action, one that did not lead the country anywhere.

Despite the workers' timidity, however, by 1986 the regime was becoming increasingly insecure about popular reaction to its policies because of sporadic worker actions and increasing resistance to its economic policies among its cadres. As noted in chapter 3, the regime resorted to a foreign exchange auction in 1986 in part to deflect increasing pressure from the urban areas. The PNDC government has also occasionally capitulated to labor demands to avoid conflict. For instance, in 1987, the government announced that it was eliminating leave allowances for employees. There was a huge uproar throughout the country; and the TUC, under severe pressure from workers, asked government to review the announcement, which it eventually did.[40] Rawlings stated that it was strategically important to concede to the workers, but he warned that "members of the military and some trained militia [are] on standby and ready to take over essential services."[41] Thus, labor acquiescence in Ghana is not based only on repression but also on the government's at least occasional ability to adopt strategies that avoid outright political conflict.

As the ERP progressed, some workers probably began to do better economically. Unfortunately, the data that the Ghana Statistical Services provide on wages are so erratic that the figures cannot be used for any type of serious analysis. Therefore, it is unclear how workers' salaries have evolved over the last few years. However, it is evident to everyone in Ghana that the overall economic situation is improving and that the regime's policies are bringing benefits—even if these benefits are not immediately concentrated among the working class. As figure 6 shows, starting in 1983, Ghana has experienced a real increase in per capita income of approximately 2 to 3 percent each year. This is a spectacular performance given that the rest of the continent, on average, has experienced an annual decline of 1 percent in per capita income.[42] Of course, Ghana is still well below where it was even in the late 1970s, but there

40. Kodwo Ewusi, "Social Welfare Theory, Structural Adjustment Policies and Labour Responses in Africa," paper presented at the International Conference on Planning for Growth and Development, Legon, March 1989, 13.

41. Quoted in "A Shameful Affair," West Africa, 5 May 1986, 920.

42. World Bank, World Development Report, 1991 (Washington, D.C.: World Bank, 1991), 207.

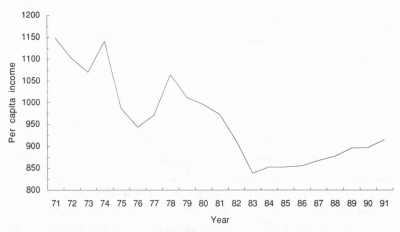

Fig. 6.   Per Capita Income during the Recovery (1985 U.S. $)

SOURCES: R. Summers and A. Heston, "The Penn World Table (Mark 5)," computer disk provided by authors; and *Enhancing the Human Impact of the Adjustment Program* (Accra: Government of Ghana, 1991), Annex Table 2.

has been enough progress to dissuade some from opposing the government. Some workers, notably those in gold mines, also are probably beginning to benefit from the upturn in their export-oriented industries that the devaluation caused. As the incomes of some workers increase, the potential popular coalition against the government weakens, making any kind of action against the government more unlikely.

Thus, through a combination of luck, repression, and political skill, the government was able to survive worker anger and implement a far-reaching economic reform program. This analysis accords with the developing conventional wisdom on economic reform, which finds that the coalition that develops to oppose cuts in subsidies and price increases during economic reform is often far less threatening than is usually imagined. For instance, Henry Bienen and Mark Gersovitz have noted that "urban food prices in African countries have in fact risen in recent years without endemic instabilities."[43]

The primary lesson of Ghana for the rest of Africa is that urban unrest cannot be predicted primarily on the basis of the severity of the economic reform program. For instance, because so few were benefiting from price controls and the overvalued exchange rate, the actual effect of the ERP on workers has probably been far less than the announcements would

43. Henry Bienen and Mark Gersovitz, "International Debt and Political Stability," *International Organization* 39, no. 4 (Autumn 1985): 753.

indicate. Because the program hurt less than it appeared to and because opposing the regime publicly could entail large costs, popular unrest was not an attractive option.

BUILDING A COALITION FOR ECONOMIC REFORM

A much more interesting question than why urban labor has not been able to protest against the PNDC is whether the ERP would ever have allowed the Rawlings regime to develop a political constituency among the workers. It can be argued that rural dwellers are the obvious constituency for the PNDC regime because so much of the ERP is devoted to promoting agriculture. However, previous Ghanaian governments sought to marginalize the rural areas, and, as chapter 5 argues, it will be very difficult in the short term to effect any kind of political mobilization among this atomized population.

In addition, the urban population continues to have the potential to riot, at least in the minds of the leaders. While I have argued that this possibility is unlikely, fear of the urban population may still weigh heavily on the minds of Ghana's rulers. Indeed, Bienen and Gersovitz argue that African leaders have consistently overestimated the likelihood of urban riots.[44] Therefore, constructing an urban constituency may have been especially important to the PNDC, which, as a regime that came to power through a coup, knows that it too can be replaced.

However, it is one of the great ironies of present-day Ghana that precisely those factors that allowed the PNDC to implement such a drastic program of economic reform in the short run created substantial obstacles to creating any constituency, much less one based on the support of workers. The PNDC during the early days of the economic reform program, when it was unclear whether it could survive the popular uproar caused by the reforms, was small, not dependent on the support of any particular group, and willing and able to use force against opponents. To create constituencies, however, the PNDC must be able to consult and build support among other groups and appear to have put aside any recourse to violence. This may have been too great a transition for the regime to make.

For instance, one way that the PNDC could have at least begun efforts at establishing a constituency among workers would have been to develop closer ties with the unions. However, in direct contrast to previous

44. Ibid.

governments, which sought to co-opt the trade unions, the PNDC did not make any effort to associate the TUC more closely with economic programs. As one senior TUC official noted in an interview, "The impression given is that the TUC is part of the planning process but it is not. Since 1983 the TUC has not been consulted. We are not in a position to participate."[45] The government was clearly wary of the TUC after its muted protests against the ERP: tolerance of criticism is not one of the personality traits of senior government officials. Given the amount of mistrust that has developed between the PNDC and official trade union structures, it would have been difficult for the government to develop a constituency among workers through the TUC.

In addition, economic reform programs create problems for regimes trying to build constituencies, as opposed to simply trying to repress groups, because there are so few popular symbols around which to rally the population. In 1982, the PNDC had some success in mobilizing workers around pledges to bring about a "revolution." However, the visible symbols of the revolution are not at all obvious now that the government is collaborating so closely with the International Monetary Fund and the World Bank. As PNDC member Mr. Justice D. F. Annan freely admitted, the "blood and thunder politics" of the early years of the PNDC are gone.[46] The obvious income disparities that have appeared, as at least some become rich under the ERP, make it clear to all Ghanaians that, whatever else, the euphoric populist policies of 1982 have now been abandoned. Indeed, Rawlings in his 1990 New Year's speech was put in what, for him, must have been the highly difficult position of defending the well-to-do:

> We need not condemn or resent all people merely for their affluence. We must acknowledge the fact that a great many people have taken full advantage of the economic conditions which the government has deliberately created to encourage individual initiative.[47]

Clearly, there was not much for the workers to rally around.

During the late 1980s, the PNDC made a concentrated effort to resurrect Nkrumah as a nationalist symbol, and there was at least some energy devoted to portraying Rawlings as Nkrumah's natural successor.

---

45. Interview, Accra, 27 September 1989.
46. Onyema-Ugochukwu, "The Lost Revolution," *West Africa*, 25 February 1985, 347.
47. Quoted in *People's Daily Graphic*, 4 January 1990.

However, this effort was extremely difficult because, just as the regime was promoting Nkrumah's legacy, it was systematically dismantling the economic measures so closely associated with Ghana's first ruler. Thus, the state enterprises that Nkrumah established to control the commanding heights of the economy were being reformed or privatized; and price controls, which were previously portrayed as helping the poor, were eliminated. When taking these actions, the regime implicitly (and correctly) tied Ghana's economic decline directly to its first leader. Therefore, Nkrumah probably cannot serve as an important symbol for workers and others to rally around.

Another avenue open to the PNDC to build a constituency among workers was through the newly created local political structures. In early 1989, voters throughout Ghana went to the polls to elect citizens to 110 newly created district assemblies. These elections were done on an individual basis, without political parties. The PNDC hoped that the district assemblies would be the beginning of a decentralized political power structure that would not revert to the political abuses of the past.

However, it was unlikely that the district assembly system, as constituted, could have been used to develop constituencies in the urban areas. The urban population in Ghana has long benefited from a political system where numbers have not counted and where geographical proximity to the leadership guaranteed that politicians would seek to purchase the urban population's quiescence. In fact, the TUC rejected the idea of district-level elections.[48] Therefore, as discussed at length in chapter 5, it is not at all surprising that the Greater Accra area had by far the lowest turnout in the election.

A reflection of the fact that any electoral system that decentralized political power would inevitably diminish the urban population's political strength was the occupational composition of the members of the assembly. Throughout the country, approximately one-third of them were peasants; another third were teachers.[49] Ghanaians were electing those who had the most in common with themselves or those who had traditionally commanded respect in the local communities. In contrast, only 40 percent of the assembly members in Greater Accra were peasants or teachers while 24 percent (twice the national average) were in the civil and public service.[50] Thus, the urban population, even in an election

48. Collen Lowe Morna, "A Grassroots Democracy," *Africa Report*, July–August 1989, 18.
49. Figures are from Ministry of Information, *Information Digest*, no. 7 (1989): 19.
50. Ibid., 19, 21.

dedicated to decentralizing political power, chose those closely associated with the state to represent them. They thereby demonstrated just
how difficult it is for a population group long used to automatically
possessing political power to begin to develop indigenous leaders apart
from the state.

The implications of the PNDC's being unable to develop an approach
whereby it gains a constituency among workers are potentially significant. Clearly, the political logic of economic reform programs is that if a
government is able to get through the immediate crisis posed by devaluation and the elimination of subsidies and price controls, it will be able to
garner increased political support in the long term as the economy
improves. However, given how reluctant the PNDC was to consult with
the TUC or to develop viable symbols around which workers could rally,
even if workers' incomes had begun to improve, it is hard to see how
those gains would have translated into political support for the Rawlings
regime. Thus, even as the economy improved, the regime remained
isolated from the urban population, with the unnerving habit of occasionally lashing out and trying to impose labor discipline—which might
have been volunteered by the unions had they been properly consulted.

CONCLUSION

The Ghanaian experience suggests that earlier examinations of the political implications of economic reform programs have fundamentally mis-
understood the dynamics of economic reform. It has not been the case in
Ghana, or many other countries, that the short-term sparks imposed by
stabilization programs have ignited wide-scale popular protests threatening to the regime. In Ghana and elsewhere in Africa, the chances of
wildcat strikes igniting urban popular protest are low and can be further
decreased by skillful government policies. However, the Rawlings regime has not been able to develop noticeable support for its policies
despite exceptional economic performance over the last few years. Thus,
as with devaluation, even a government that successfully raises prices
may not be able to develop long-term support for fundamental changes
in institutional structures. Indeed, the very success in raising prices may
have seriously compromised the structural adjustment effort.

CHAPTER 5

Is There a
Rural Constituency
for Economic Reform?

Ghana adopted poor economic policies because leaders were desperately searching to establish and enhance political constituencies that would allow them to retain power. In particular, policies (including the exchange rate, price controls, and subsidies on key commodities) were biased to keep the politically important urban class quiescent and to enrich the state. As J. Dirck Stryker and his colleagues noted, "It was the failure of politics to provide an effective mechanism for influencing policy in the allocation of resources that led ultimately to the collapse of the regime."[1] The problem facing Ghana and other African countries that hope to adopt comprehensive economic reform programs is to develop political systems in which politicians do not have incentives to introduce ruinous policies with an urban bias for political gain. In particular, Ghana will have to develop a system whereby the rural population has a political voice significant enough to be a viable constituency for the economic reform policies now being adopted. Indeed, the World Bank now stresses the lack of "countervailing power" as one of the key elements of Africa's "crisis of governance."[2]

In addition, the question of a peasant constituency is important to the long-term sustainability of economic reform. As will be noted in chapter 6, the World Bank does not have a model of how political systems evolve

1. J. Dirck Stryker, *Trade, Exchange Rate, and Agricultural Pricing Policies in Ghana* (Washington, D.C.: World Bank, 1990), 263.
2. World Bank, *Sub-Saharan Africa: From Crisis to Sustainable Growth* (Washington, D.C.: World Bank, 1989), 60.

while African states reform—although there is a clear though untested assumption that as economies grow and the welfare of individuals improves, political support for the regime and for continued reform will develop. In this model, economic improvement generates almost immediate political support. Of course, this assumption becomes even more important given the problems that Ghana, and probably many other African countries, will have when trying to develop constituencies in the urban areas.

Unfortunately, the implied political model ignores several factors. First, other barriers, especially long-standing ethnic hostilities, may obstruct the deterministic progression from economic improvement to political support. Second, large transaction costs prevent quick changes in the nature of constituency support. Third, the implied model of political support in economic reform models ignores the institutional requirements for the development of political constituencies. Indeed, this chapter will argue that for political support to be meaningfully transmitted to national leaders, the PNDC or other reforming regimes will have to develop far more dense political institutions in the rural areas than Ghana or most other African countries have ever had.

Some scholars have already asserted that the PNDC probably cannot generate a rural constituency strong enough to replace the urban one it is losing.[3] If Ghana cannot develop a constituency for the policies it has adopted since 1983, one of three things will eventually occur: The leadership could respond to perceived pressures from the urban population by adopting the counterproductive practices of the past, which bought city-dweller support at the price of faulty national economic policies. Or the country might have to remain under the permanent tutelage of the World Bank and the International Monetary Fund, the only two organizations in Ghana presently capable of providing a political counterweight to the urban population. Finally, the alignment of political constituencies could remain largely unchanged even though agricultural policies favoring the peasantry would continue, primarily because of the preferences of the leadership.

The question of whether a constituency for structural adjustment can be established also immediately intersects with a whole series of questions about political structures and the prospects for democracy in Africa. As Larry Diamond has noted, "Virtually everywhere in Africa,

3. Gwendolyn Mikell, "Peasant Politicisation and Economic Recuperation in Ghana: Local and National Dilemmas," *Journal of Modern African Studies* 27 (September 1989): 477.

the formal political arena has remained narrow, even when it has not been narrowed as a deliberate authoritarian strategy."[4] A constituency for structural adjustment based in the rural areas would therefore be a strikingly different development for countries such as Ghana. In addition, while a system giving the rural population more political voice would not necessarily have to be one in which votes counted, empowering the rural population is clearly a crucial step in the slow process of democratization.

This chapter will also examine the equally important question of the ability of an African government to develop a system of local administration so that information concerning developments in the rural areas can be transmitted to the central government. The type of urban, centralized systems of rule that Ghana and other African governments have are information poor because they do not encourage the transmittal of prices, demands, and other sources of information from the rural areas. There is no need for this type of information if a government's constituency is in the urban areas and its economic policies ignore the rural areas. However, a government with an orientation toward the rural areas needs information from areas beyond the cities. Also, a government that adopts sound economic policies needs information about the entire economy, not just that of the urban areas, if it is to rehabilitate roads, distribute seeds and fertilizer, build schools and clinics, and the like. The flow of information is thus a particularly important political question for those governments trying to move from stabilization to structural adjustment.

THE DISEMPOWERED RURAL POPULATION

The disempowerment of the rural population is both a political given that confronts African leaders and a consequence of the authoritarian and centralizing actions of governments in the colonial and postcolonial periods. First, poor roads and telecommunications systems in all African countries cause the rural population to seem even more distant from the capital than they really are and also make it difficult for the peasantry to organize among themselves. Second, the atomistic nature of the peasantry, especially their large numbers and low individual output, poses exceptional barriers to organization. As Robert Bates notes, it is much

---

4. Larry Diamond, "Introduction: Roots of Failure, Seeds of Hope," in *Democracy in Developing Countries: Africa*, ed. Larry Diamond, Juan J. Linz, and Seymour Martin Lipset (Boulder: Lynne Rienner, 1988), 19.

easier for an industry—in which only a few players are involved—to organize than a peasantry that, as in the case of Ghana, numbers more than seven million, because the benefits from organization will be divided over such a large number of people that it will not be worthwhile for anyone to attempt to organize.[5]

In addition, rulers in African states have taken many steps to further marginalize the population over the last few decades. During colonial rule, no effort was devoted to developing political systems whereby the rural population could have significant voice. Postcolonial African governments also hindered empowerment of the rural population. Nkrumah, for instance, tried to co-opt the burgeoning cocoa farmers' movement by absorbing it into his Conventions People's Party.[6]

Governments have also used force to crush political organizations in the rural areas because these movements could become the basis of opposition politics. This was notably the case in Ghana when the National Liberation Movement (NLM) advocated the secession of Ashanti region during the 1950s in response to the government's inadequate cocoa prices. As Bates notes,

> The fate of the NLM in Ghana and the KPU [Kenya People's Union] in Kenya is paralleled by the fate of opposition parties in a host of other African nations. Because the majority of the African people live in rural areas, it is inevitable that their fate becomes central in the appeals of any political opposition. With the use of the state's instruments of coercion to emasculate the political opposition, governments in power thus eliminate one of the basic elements of political life which, by the sheer weight of self-interested political calculation, would champion the interests of the rural majority.[7]

Precisely because governments have so little information about what is happening in the rural areas, they react harshly to any indication of a threatening political development. They have neither the knowledge nor the political systems to develop a more nuanced approach to rural unrest.

In addition, very few African countries have long-standing political systems in which votes count. In Ghana, for instance, the three attempts at civilian rule have all ended in military coups. The failure to develop political systems in which numbers translate into political power is obviously detrimental to the rural peasantry who account for, in Ghana

5. This is a major theme in Robert H. Bates, *Markets and States in Tropical Africa* (Berkeley: University of California Press, 1981), 89.

6. See Björn Beckman, *Organising the Farmers: Cocoa Politics and National Development in Ghana* (Uppsala: Scandinavian Institute of African Studies, 1976).

7. Bates, *Markets and States*, 107–8.

and most other African countries, more than 70 percent of the population. Where sheer numbers do not translate into political strength, it is almost inevitable that groups such as the urban population, numerically quite small but able to threaten the leadership through physical violence, come to dominate political systems.

But even democratic rule, where the rural population might have possessed greater political power because of their sheer numbers, did not bring substantial empowerment of smallholders in Ghana. As the National Commission for Democracy noted,

> Each of our constitutional experiments failed because the type of representational system we adopted on each occasion made governments remote and distant from the primary communities that were alleged to have elected them. Consequently governments remained in the hands of a few, and above all represented the interest of the economically powerful who had access to these resources.[8]

Therefore, independent Ghana has never come close to having the institutions necessary to allow the formation of a rural constituency for economic reform.

Finally, the years of economic decline and, somewhat paradoxically, the manner in which the reform program has been implemented, have further marginalized the rural population. As Ghana's administrative system fell apart in the 1970s and early 1980s, the rural population was further distanced from the state. Those elements of the state present in the rural areas—extension agents, marketing organizations, district offices—simply stopped working as the Ghanaian state imploded and civil servants could do little more than try to fend for themselves. The peasant population was increasingly left to conduct farming for self-sufficiency and little more.

The extremely narrow base with which the PNDC came to power then had the effect of continuing to exclude the rural population. Especially immediately after the coup, the leadership's attention was devoted to mobilizing the urban population. Hansen is right to note that "there was no attempt to mobilise them [the peasantry] although there were important local issues and grievances around which they could be mobilised in support of the regime and their own independent class interests."[9] This exclusion continued for several years as the narrowly formed

8. National Commission for Democracy, *The Search for True Democracy in Ghana* (Accra: Information Services Department [1990?]), 1.
9. Emmanuel Hansen, "The State and Popular Struggles in Ghana, 1982–1986," in *Popular Struggles for Democracy in Africa*, ed. Peter Anyang' Nyong'o (London: United Nations University, 1987), 176, 191.

PNDC focused on implementing the initial stabilization program. Even when the PNDC began to move to reform fundamental economic institutions, however, it had such a narrow political base and so few links to the rural population that it could not easily develop any kind of contact with the peasantry. Once again, how the early reforms were implemented would have severe implications for the politics of medium- and long-term economic reform.

EFFORTS TO PROMOTE AGRICULTURE IN GHANA

Ghana is a particularly interesting case to examine the construction of political constituencies in rural areas because the Economic Recovery Programme has had, as one of its central pillars since 1983, the promotion of agriculture. In the first few years of the program, cocoa received most of the attention, to the relative neglect of food crops. Cocoa was the backbone of the economy and had to be revived if the economy was going to prosper. As Dr. Abbey noted, "In the early years survival itself was at stake. The country was perilously close to collapse. We faced the prospect of social-political collapse."[10] Also, the IMF's focus on the current account imbalance may have made policymakers especially eager to reinvigorate their major export. At the same time, given the very limited administrative abilities of the Ghanaian government, it may not have been possible for the government to focus on more than one area in agriculture.

The first policy measure to affect cocoa was the devaluation, which had the immediate effect of increasing the cedi price of cocoa. Nominal prices also were increased and, as the Cocoa Marketing Board was reformed, cocoa farmers began to receive a higher percentage of the world price. Just between 1984 and 1988, the nominal price of cocoa increased fivefold. The Structural Adjustment Credit with the World Bank called upon the government to provide cocoa farmers with 55 percent of the international price by 1988/1989.[11] Cocoa production, which bottomed out at 158,000 tons in 1983, is projected to average approximately 300,000 tons in the early 1990s (figure 7).

It was not until the PNDC began to review the country's progress, in the run-up to the second phase of the ERP in 1986, that a focus on food agriculture emerged. The country was fortunate that in 1984 there had

10. Interview, London, 20 August 1990.
11. Simon Commander, John Howell, and Wayone Seini, "Ghana: 1983–1987," in *Structural Adjustment & Agriculture,* ed. Simon Commander (London: Overseas Development Institute, 1989), 112.

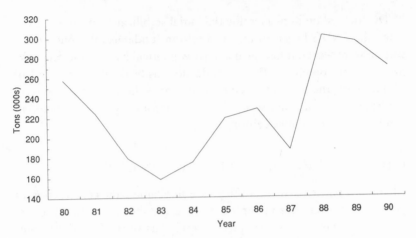

Fig. 7.   Cocoa Production during the Recovery
  SOURCES: K. Ewusi, *Statistical Tables on the Economy of Ghana* (Legon: Institute of
Statistical, Social, and Economic Research, 1986); and Commodity Research Bureau, *CRB
Commodity Yearbook, 1991* (New York: CRB, 1991).

been good rains to increase agricultural production, but it was obvious
that the ad hoc measures taken up to that point could not guarantee an
adequate food supply. A number of initiatives were therefore taken
under the Agriculture Sector Review to strengthen the institutional
framework of the agricultural policy sector, improve the delivery of
public-sector services to agriculture, and enhance the distribution of
agricultural inputs. For the period 1990–1995, the government has
begun implementing the Medium-Term Agricultural Development Programme, which seeks to increase food crop output and to create a more
balanced agricultural sector. Table 1 displays the government's ambitious goals for 1995. Overall, agriculture is projected to grow at a rate
of 4.7 percent a year.[12] If these ambitious targets are met, grain production will be doubled. As a result, food, which now accounts for 80
percent of current incomes, will decrease to 60 percent of total incomes
by 1995.[13]
     Ghana is therefore in the process of massively changing the incentives
for agricultural producers. Indeed, at least for cocoa, the urban-rural
terms of trade seem to have reverted to the level they were in the early

    12. Ministry of Agriculture, *Medium Term Agricultural Development Program* (Ac-
cra: Government Printers, 1990), 80.
    13. PNDC, *Achievement of the PNDC in the Agricultural Sector under Ghana's
Economic Recovery Programme (1983–1988)*, May 1989, 21.

TABLE 1   FOOD CROP OUTPUT
(tons/hectare)

Crop	Yield in 1988	Projected Yield, 1995
Cassava	5–6	10
Yam	4.5–5	7
Plantain	5–6	8
Cocoyam	5–6	7
Maize	1–1.2	2.5
Rice	.8–1.2	2.0
Sorghum	.8–1.0	2.0
Millet	.6–.8	1.5
Postharvest Loss	20%–30%	10%–15%

SOURCE: PNDC, *Achievement of the PNDC in the Agricultural Sector under Ghana's Economic Recovery Programme (1983–1988),* May 1989, 20.

1970s.[14] On a symbolic level also it has been clear that the ERP has been biased toward the rural areas. Indeed, Rawlings's central indictment against the old regime is that it exploited the farmers. In 1983 he said,

> Cocoa and forest products make up about 75 percent of all our export receipts and yet the benefits you get from the system [are] small in comparison with what you put in. It is with your agricultural products that we buy the cars, lorries, petrol, kerosene, matches, soap, sugar, etc. and yet how many of you have access to these things? We intend to reverse this trend and bring back the wealth of the country to where it belongs, in the rural areas.[15]

However, it should be noted that people in the rural areas are still absolutely poorer than they were in the mid-1970s (much less than at independence) and will be for some time to come. Although cocoa production increased from 158,000 tons in 1983 to 270,000 tons in 1990, and although there is significant evidence that farmers are finally planting new cocoa trees,[16] significant income gains for cocoa farmers will only appear slowly because it takes seven years for the trees to yield a

14. W. Asenso Okyere, "The Response of Farmers to Ghana's Adjustment Policies," in *Working Papers: The Long-Term Perspective Study of Sub-Saharan Africa,* vol. 2 (Washington, D.C.: World Bank, 1990), 78–79.

15. J. J. Rawlings, "Boosting the Morale of Farmers," in *Forging Ahead* (Tema: Ghana Publishing Corporation, 1983), 4.

16. Commodity Research Bureau, *CRB Commodity Yearbook, 1991* (New York: CRB, 1991), 35.

crop. The recent dramatic increase in cocoa sales does not indicate a gain in farmers' income of a similar magnitude because much of the "new" production is actually from cocoa that had previously been diverted to Côte d'Ivoire. In the food-growing areas, it will also be some time before farmers experience significant income gains. Inevitably, gains for these smallholders will be halting and will vary widely depending on the region as the state starts to reconstruct its agricultural system. Therefore, it is important not to overestimate the immediate effects of the ERP on rural people in Ghana. Indeed, one of the tests of the ERP will be whether or not it can construct a constituency while only slowly increasing the real incomes of rural people.

Similarly, government efforts to establish more administrative structures in the rural areas have met with very little success. Especially in light of the mixed economic prospects of the rural areas, there is no evidence at present that the regime has the institutional structures to cultivate a rural constituency or to gather significant amounts of information about what is happening in the rural areas. Research by students of the University of Ghana, Legon, on the Committees for the Defence of the Revolution (CDR) and their predecessors, the WDCs and the PDCs, suggests that most of the organizations the Rawlings government has attempted to establish in the rural areas are disorganized and ineffective. Augustus Opong Ansah's conclusion that the CDR had all but collapsed in Akwapim district is supported by many other studies and by anecdotal evidence.[17] More generally, despite the government's rhetoric of trying to reach out to the peasantry, to many government officials, the majority of Ghanaians still live in a different world. As one Ministry of Finance official noted in an interview,

> Society has been unfortunately organized. Peasants are organized around an old societal structure while government is organized around a modern administrative machinery. We observe two different decision-making processes going on as if they were opposed to each other. Peasants see government differently from the organizational point of view. We have not succeeded in integrating the two organizations.[18]

17. Augustus Opong Ansah, "The CDR's since December 31st 1981: The Case of Akwapim District," Honors Thesis, University of Ghana, Legon, 1986, 48. See also Attan Makamadu, "The CDR Concept: A Rural/Urban Analysis: A Comparative Case Study of Nanumba District and Accra District," Honors Thesis, University of Ghana, Legon, 1987; Kwasi Ofori-Yeboah, "CDR's and Political Change in Ghana since the 31st December Revolution: A Case Study of Madina," Honors Thesis, University of Ghana, Legon, 1987; Douglas Doyki Kissi, "The CDR's, Political Change and the Grassroots Democracy in Ghana—The Case of the Kwabu District," Honors Thesis, University of Ghana, Legon, 1987.

18. Interview, Accra, 25 September 1989.

There are still many indications in Ghana that the rural areas are viewed as bastions of backwardness and that true economic growth is associated with industrialization in the urban areas.

Thus, while the government indicates that it wants the peasants to have a greater voice, it has yet to take substantive actions to allow them a greater input into the policy process. For instance, the government has not aided the establishment of a nationwide peasant organization, which would provide smallholders with a visible political presence in the capital through which they could influence policy.

In contrast, the Zimbabwe government has given aid to peasant farmer groups so that they will at least be a visible part of the policy process.[19] The Zimbabwe government was able to include the peasant association in the policy-making process because the setting of prices for crops is an open process in which farmers have an institutionalized voice. In contrast, the PNDC's deliberations are not open to this kind of participation from societal groups. More generally, it is simply not the style of Rawlings and his colleagues in the PNDC, especially after a decade of authoritarian rule, to self-consciously try to open up the political process. Therefore, the government has not felt the urge to encourage peasants to create national structures that would attempt to influence the policy-making process. As one Ministry of Agriculture official said to me,

> Farmers have no comparative advantage in formulating policies. They have a comparative advantage in production. There is not a one to one relationship between farmer participation and their improved productivity. Improved extension and ensuring adequate supply of inputs at the doorstep is more important for productivity.[20]

On a material and symbolic level, the government has announced that it intends that the benefits of structural adjustment be focused on the rural areas. However, the economic benefits will be slow to come to the rural areas. It will certainly not appear to many rural people that there has been a dramatic improvement in the standards of living directly tied to government action. In addition, the PNDC has run into a host of administrative and attitudinal problems commonly found throughout Africa. Therefore, it is particularly appropriate to ask if the benefits that the PNDC have promised to deliver to the rural areas can create a rural constituency for structural adjustment and how the rural areas might

19. See Jeffrey Herbst, *State Politics in Zimbabwe* (Berkeley: University of California Press, 1990), chap. 5.
20. Interview, Accra, 10 August 1989.

express support for the government. Inevitably, given the changes in terms of trade, it is also important to ask if the increase in support in the rural areas will be enough to overcome the political damage resulting from the urban populations' relative material deprivation.

THE ETHNIC OVERLAY

Constructing rural constituencies is not simply a question of distributing greater resources to the rural areas. In Ghana, as in most other African countries, leaders are linked to a variety of constituencies through geography, ethnicity, and class. In Ghana, a particularly important factor that must be reviewed is the ethnic split between the PNDC and the majority of the rural population. This ethnic split is especially relevant because it divides the PNDC from the group that has apparently benefited the most from the structural reform efforts: the largely Ashanti cocoa farmers in the middle forest belt of the country. This ethnic division adds an extra, important dimension to questions posed above because it must now be asked if the PNDC can form a constituency for structural adjustment despite an ethnic cleavage that has been an integral part of Ghanaian politics since independence. Consideration of the ethnic factor also makes the examination of the potential for constructing rural constituencies much more realistic than political models that simplistically assume that greater incomes translate into more political support.

Since 1957, ethnicity in Ghana has been an extraordinarily rich pattern of shifting coalitions. Nominally, approximately 44 percent of the country (largely in the middle) belong to the major Akan configuration (Asante, Fante, Brong, Akim, Nzima); the Mole-Dagbani group (northern) constitute 16 percent; the Ewe (southeast) 13 percent; the Ga-Adangbe (Accra region) 8.3 percent; and other groups roughly 17 percent.[21] For the purposes of this discussion, the dynamics of the Ashanti grouping are particularly important because this group tends to dominate the cocoa-producing regions in the country and, with memories of the National Liberation Movement still vivid in many people's minds, poses particular problems for any government trying to develop a rural constituency.[22]

The Ashanti question becomes especially important because the PNDC is in reality, and, more important, is largely perceived as being,

21. Figures are from Naomi Chazan, "Ethnicity and Politics in Ghana," *Political Science Quarterly* 97 (Fall 1982): 462.

22. Dennis Austin, *Politics in Ghana, 1946–1960* (London: Oxford University Press, 1964), 253–57.

Ewe-based. Unfortunately, given the highly depoliticized nature of Ghanaian society, it is almost impossible to gauge how salient the Ewe-Ashanti conflict is to the population at large. Certainly, there has been elite protest at what is seen as Ewe domination of the PNDC. As Professor A. Adu Boahen noted in his Danquah lecture,

> Whether Rawlings is aware of this or not, this situation [all top government positions being held by Ewes] is giving the unfortunate impression that the country is being dominated and ruled by that single ethnic group, and this impression is causing . . . anger and irritation.[23]

Unfortunately, Professor Boahen's analysis was about the only cogent political critique of the PNDC in the 1980s. However, Kumasi elites interviewed often expressed similar sentiments in private. For instance, it was the feeling of one group that the PNDC was "the most tribalized government" Ghana had ever had.[24]

Indeed, comments like this are common, even though Kumasi and Ashanti region have benefited from the economic upturn since 1983. As one senior community official said,

> The Region [Ashanti] feels discriminated against. People see the Kumasi-Accra road but that is also the Kumasi-Tamale road. People feel that projects which have been established in Ashanti have been done with wealth from the region—especially the cocoa which pays the East German firms for the roads—but that other regions get aid. People in Ashanti Region do not feel they are getting their fair share.[25]

Beyond the impression of elite unhappiness, however, it is extremely difficult to gauge popular feeling in Ashanti region, or anywhere else in Ghana, toward the PNDC. As one journalist noted,

> There is nothing you can do [about politics] but enjoy it. You cannot agitate. People present their petitions at durbars but that is it. Everyone is suffering from the squeeze. There is nothing else you can do but to tighten belts and go into farming or petty trading. In the absence of political parties there is no way that you can agitate politically. There is no organized means of raising political issues.[26]

As these interviews make clear, the ethnic tension between people in Ashanti region and the PNDC is a clear barrier to creating rural constitu-

---

23. A. Adu Boahen, *The Ghanaian Sphinx* (Accra: Ghana Academy of Arts and Sciences, 1989), 53.
24. Interview, 7 February 1990. Obviously, it is particularly important to respect interview confidentiality on this issue.
25. Interview, Kumasi, 9 February 1990.
26. Interview, 7 February 1990.

encies for economic reform. Even though the increase in economic activity has been palpable in the region, many in Kumasi attribute (to some degree, correctly) most of the development to the resources the region itself generates. In some cases, the overall animosity toward the Ewe-based regime causes some citizens to simply ignore the welfare gains they may have experienced. Of course, even after many years of economic reform, the gains in Ashanti region are not overwhelming, and many people recognize that they were better off in the 1970s. That Ghana may have been unable to grow any faster is of little consequence to people who are absolutely poor. Even in Ashanti region, the area that has unquestionably benefited the most from the PNDC's economic policies, there is no clear link between improvement in overall economic aggregates and clear political support. Indeed, there is some indication that even if economic conditions become substantially better in Ashanti region, people will not automatically give their support to the Rawlings government.

The inability to accurately gauge popular opinion in Ashanti region is particularly important to note because the government faces the same problem. Because previous governments and the PNDC have effectively removed all channels of political communication between the urban state and the rural masses for such a long time, it is exceptionally difficult for the leadership to measure support of or opposition to their own policies, especially in an area that is seen as ethnically hostile. Indeed, PNDC officials picture themselves as being only loosely connected to the popular pulse in regions such as Ashanti and are only truly aware that something is going wrong when there is mass political dissension or after grumbling from local CDR officials reaches such a pitch that it makes itself heard in the PNDC. The PNDC can hear the drums beat, but they do not know what those drums mean.

BUILDING NEW CONSTITUENCIES: THE DISTRICT ASSEMBLIES

The more perceptive PNDC officials recognized that the organizational structure under which they took power could not continue indefinitely if they were actually to undertake a program of economic reform. A government of a dozen policymakers could withstand the popular onslaught caused by cuts in subsidies and devaluation, but it cannot create a system that would cultivate a rural constituency supportive of a long, comprehensive economic reform program. As PNDC member P. V.

Obeng noted, "We realised that we had not been able to tap the ingenuity and resources at grassroots effectively to back the national thrust for recovery, we had to decide how to do so."[27]

Therefore, in 1988, the PNDC began to decentralize the government. First, it created a series of 110 district assemblies. It was widely recognized in Ghana that these district assemblies would not be the end of governmental reform; the assemblies had no real powers, and it was particularly unclear what demands they could legitimately press on the central government. However, the PNDC rejected attempting elections similar to those that inaugurated the Busia and Liman regimes. Indeed, senior Ghanaian officials are critical of efforts at democratization, such as Nigeria's, that focus on creating national organizations (e.g., two major political parties) rather than a local base for democracy. In particular, they feel that such efforts are incompatible with economic reform. Top governmental officials believe that a system beginning at the grass roots is more likely to succeed than is one imposed from above.

The Rawlings regime therefore sponsored elections to the district assemblies in three phases during 1988 and 1989. Only individuals were allowed to run for election; no parties or other forms of organized political support were allowed formally to express themselves. In addition, the PNDC reserved the right to appoint up to one-third of the members of the district assemblies. Nevertheless, the district assemblies exercise succeeded in attracting a significant turnout, especially compared to recent elections (table 2). Even in the independence election of 1956, only 50 percent of the eligible voters cast ballots.[28]

However, it is impossible to read the overall turnout figures as a victory for the PNDC. Some who voted obviously supported the PNDC, but there may have been many others who voted in order to hasten the day when the PNDC left office to be replaced by a democratically elected government. Given that approximately 2,200 separate elections were held for the 110 district assemblies, a large number of local factors undoubtedly influenced the turnout figures. For instance, there were certainly politicians from the parties that had ruled Ghana previously who suggested that if their supporters came out in large numbers, it would be the first step to reinstalling those parties in power, precisely what the PNDC did not want.

27. Quoted in Ad'Obe Obe, "Managing a Revolution," West Africa, 11 March 1990, 360.
28. Austin, Politics, 347.

TABLE 2   COMPARATIVE VOTER TURNOUT
(percentages)

Region	1988–1989 District Assembly	1979 Parliamentary	1978 Council
Western	55.3	34.04	20.6
Central	59.3	33.34	22.2
Eastern	60.8	35.95	16.6
Volta	59.4	33.65	15.3
Ashanti	60.8	41.99	24.9
Brong/Ahafo	60.2	33.16	18.7
Northern	60.6	32.09	18.2
Upper[a]	65.7	32.82	16.1
Greater Accra	44.3	35.59	10.2
Nation	59.0	35.25	18.4

SOURCES: Ministry of Local Government, *Information Digest,* no. 5 (1989), 3; and Ministry of Information, *Information Digest,* special edition (1989), 4.
[a]The PNDC had divided Upper Region into Upper West and Upper East. The results from these two regions are combined here so they can be compared to previous elections.

The high turnout figures can be read simply as reflecting strong sentiment among the largely rural population in Ghana in favor of political structures that might decentralize political power. Kojo T-Vieta is correct to note that "the high turnout in rural areas and newly created districts can be attributed to effective PNDC propaganda for District Assemblies as powerful vehicles for local development. New districts took the elections as a serious opportunity to catch up with old districts."[29] The district assemblies elections were, most of all, a referendum on the district assemblies.

The district assemblies, however, cannot actually shift the balance of power in Ghanaian politics because they are not systematically tied to the central government in any manner. For instance, there is no procedure whereby they can make resource demands on specific ministries. Nor do they have the ability to allocate resources or raise taxes. Correspondingly, the central government has not yet even begun to modify national ministries so that they can be responsive to demands emanating from rural areas. Given the disarray of many of the national ministries,

29. "Mixed Results," *West Africa,* 3 April 1989, 511.

which do not have the administrative strength to meet the problems they face now, restructuring them to be responsive to the rural areas will be a significant challenge. Most of the national leadership recognizes that the district assemblies are a long way from providing the PNDC with the kind of institutional conduits needed to have a true rural constituency.

In addition, the PNDC faces the problem that apolitical organizations such as the district assemblies cannot be expected to provide political support. The PNDC has gone out of its way to say that the district assemblies will not operate as previous civilian regimes did and that they will not be divided along party lines. Rather, government officials argue that for the peasantry, politics and government "are about how to improve their mud-houses, their drinking water, their capacity to bring their farm produce to the market-place, have their health needs attended to and have schools for their children."[30]

However, the PNDC cannot have it both ways: it cannot prevent district assembly members from organizing around political positions but somehow expect that a rural constituency will automatically emerge from these assemblies. Only if the PNDC takes the lid off politics in the rural areas will there be any chance for a real rural constituency to develop. For instance, Joel Barkan argues that because of frequent, consequential elections in Kenya, the state was held accountable to the peasantry through a series of patron-client ties.[31] In Ghana, however, the PNDC has so far been unwilling to liberalize politics because it fears that liberalization will generate opposition and because its operating style has been to deny political expression as much as possible. The best indication of the unwillingness of the PNDC to contemplate real politics in the rural areas has been its insistence on appointing a significant number of people to each district assembly; such appointees, it is assumed, will be beholden to the central government rather than responsive to constituents.

Another "defect" in the system is that there is no way in which the district assemblies can transmit information from the rural areas to the national leadership. The assemblies are not designed to transmit information, and they currently lack the expertise or the resources to competently survey their constituencies even if they desired to inform the

30. D. F. Annan, *Statement on National Economic Programme and District Level Elections* (Accra: Information Services Department, 1987), 3.

31. Joel D. Barkan, "The Electoral Process and Peasant-State Relations in Kenya," in *Elections in Independent Africa*, ed. Fred M. Hayward (Boulder: Westview, 1987), 213–15.

central government about the state of agriculture, the roads, or social services. Also, the central government itself does not have the capability at this time to begin to absorb significant information from the countryside, even if there were a dense enough institutional structure to transmit greater amounts of data.

REQUIREMENTS FOR AN ECONOMIC REFORM CONSTITUENCY

A government in Ghana, or in most other African countries, that had a strong rural constituency would have to operate on something of a paradoxical basis: it would have to be strong enough to physically resist the urban population should city-dwellers try to exercise their political opposition through physical violence, but flexible enough to decentralize a significant amount of government administration to the local level. It would also have to be responsive to a large amount of sometimes confusing information coming in from the countryside. It is the need for this difficult amalgam of authoritarian practice and democratic receptiveness that has fueled the endless, and largely unproductive, debates on whether it is best to have a democratic or authoritarian government implement dramatic economic reforms. No matter what a regime calls itself, it must have aspects of both if it is to implement significant economic reform.

As argued in chapter 4, for a variety of reasons the PNDC does have the ability to keep the urban population from threatening its rule. Indeed, given that the Rawlings regime survived the traumatic early years of the Economic Recovery Programme, the government is unlikely to be toppled by a dramatic popular uprising sparked by economic grievances. This situation is fine for stabilization but, as noted above, becomes increasingly inadequate as the country tries to reform basic institutions.

A future Ghana government could, of course, eventually design a system of local government that would provide a significant amount of information concerning developments in the rural areas. This system would have to be considerably more than the district assemblies, which are not presently connected to the central government in any systematic way. If regional organizations were established as intermediaries between the central Accra government and the district assemblies, however, it is conceivable that the assemblies could generate significant amounts of usable information. Of course, reformed district assemblies would also have to be assigned real duties and some funds from the central government if they are to become more than local debating societies.

Unfortunately, it is much more likely that denser rural institutional structures will be haphazardly created as economic reform increasingly affects the rural areas. Much time and energy will therefore be lost as the government tries to design institutions to catch up to its expanding information needs. Given the administrative disarray the PNDC inherited and its style of rule, perhaps nothing more could be expected from it. However, it is a clear lesson for future governments that lack of institutions in the rural areas to transmit information will have a strong impact on the design and implementation of policy as structural adjustment continues.

CONCLUSION

It is clear that even after eight years of structural adjustment, the PNDC cannot look to the rural areas for strong political support to reform the economy. Whether the PNDC or a government similar to it—unelected, with an obvious ethnic bias, and run by a relatively small group of officials—could actually attract outright support from the rural areas is less clear, and at this point unknowable. Too many questions are unanswerable given the level of information available to outside observers or government officials in Accra: Have the economic improvement and the prospects for moderate growth in the future caused rural dwellers to change attitudes developed toward the state during the long period of decline? How important is the lack of democratic practices to the rural population if its economic plight is improving? Does capturing political support require just a general improvement in the economic environment, or does it also depend on the allocation of specific goods (e.g., roads, factories) to tie groups specifically to the leadership (a method tried by past Ghanaian governments)? As this book indicates, the very approach to stabilization that the Rawlings government took makes winning political support during structural adjustment extremely difficult.

It should not be assumed that a democratic successor government to the PNDC would automatically be able to cultivate a rural constituency that would be instrumental in providing support for structural adjustment. As noted earlier, previous democratic experiments in Ghana and Nigeria, among other countries, did not result in rural empowerment. Whether the new wave of democratization sweeping Africa will empower the countryside is unclear; the democracy movement in Ghana and in the other African countries seems largely to be an urban affair. Finally, this chapter has stressed that, irrespective of initial attitudes that reforming politicians might have, the severely limited institutional presence of most African states in the countryside poses real barriers to cultivating peasant support for reform. Elections that matter may be only a first step in reorienting African governments to the countryside during the reform process. Chapter 9 will argue that a host of other political reforms—notably, the freedom to form political associations—must also be accomplished before elections can be expected to fundamentally change the political terms of trade between the cities and the countryside. Certainly, it should be recognized that the assumption that even relatively dramatic economic growth will lead automatically to the creation of a rural constituency for reform is simplistic.

CHAPTER 6

The Economic Frontiers of the African State

A central goal of economic reform in Ghana and in other African countries is to bring about fundamental changes in the state apparatus. This is a particularly contentious issue because many arguments over economic reform in Africa revolve around differing assumptions about the economic frontiers of the state. So far, most of the public debate concerning the future economic role of the state in Africa has focused on issues involving privatization because divestiture is a controversial reform that invokes strong emotions and has received a great deal of publicity. However, privatization is not the central issue in determining the future borders of the state in Ghana or elsewhere in Africa because privatization per se is not grounded in a basic view of what the state should or should not do.

Indeed, the effort to change the state in economic reform programs across Africa so far has been driven primarily by short-term concerns about fiscal balances rather than by a well-founded vision of the economic frontiers of the state. The more basic issue of what the state should do in Ghana and the rest of Africa still needs to be addressed. Without a well-developed view of the state, efforts to reform the state apparatus in Africa will inevitably be held captive to ever-shifting ideological fads with the result that much time and effort will be wasted.[1]

Understanding the frontiers of the state is particularly important

1. For an argument that current views will change, see Tony Killick, "Twenty-Five Years in Development: The Rise and Impending Decline of Market Solutions," *Development Policy Review* 4 (June 1986).

because there appears to be a sharp contrast between the suggestions of the World Bank and the IMF regarding the economic role of the state and the emerging view of the state in the highly successful countries of East Asia. Those financial institutions, as discussed below, appear to favor a general shrinkage of the state and a reduction of its overall involvement in the economy. In contrast, the states in East Asia are not only large, but they appear to intervene extensively in their economies. For instance, Chalmers Johnson, in his important study of Japan, approvingly quotes a former vice-minister of the Ministry of International Trade and Industry (MITI) as saying, "It is an utterly self-centered [businessman's] point of view to think that the government should be concerned with providing only a favorable environment for industries without telling them what to do."[2] Similarly, Alice H. Amsden argues in her study of South Korea that a crucial aspect of development among late industrializers is that "the state intervenes with subsidies deliberately to distort relative prices to stimulate economic activity."[3] The South Korean state also intervened massively in many sectors to help promote growth. Thus, "Hyundai was nominated as sole maker of marine engines, Kia was ordered to cease car making, and Daewoo marine-engine manufacturing; fifty-three of the sixty-eight shipping companies were collapsed into sixteen."[4] Robert Wade has also persuasively demonstrated that highly interventionist sectoral policies were critical to industrialization in both Taiwan and South Korea.[5] Clearly, the paths of the paradigmatic Third World success stories seem to contradict the general thrust of advice from the World Bank concerning the relationship between market and state.

Finally, examining the economic role of the state immediately raises one of the central questions in political science: "who, whom?" That is, "who plans whom, who directs and dominates whom, who assigns to other people their station in life, and who is to have his due allotted by others?"[6] Unfortunately, public choice analysis, the type of inquiry most

2. Chalmers Johnson, *MITI and the Japanese Miracle* (Stanford: Stanford University Press, 1982), 9–10.
3. Alice H. Amsden, *Asia's Next Giant: South Korea and Late Industrialization* (New York: Oxford University Press, 1989), 8.
4. Nigel Harris, *The End of the Third World: Newly Industrializing Countries and the Decline of an Ideology* (London: Penguin, 1986), 42.
5. Robert Wade, "Industrial Policy in East Asia: Does It Lead or Follow the Market?" in *Manufacturing Miracles: Paths of Industrialization in Latin America and East Asia*, ed. Gary Gereffi and Donald L. Wyman (Princeton: Princeton University Press, 1990), 260–61.
6. The phrase was coined by Disraeli. The quote is from F. A. Hayek, *The Road to Serfdom* (London: Routledge & Kegan Paul, 1976), 81.

commonly associated with explorations of the economic frontiers of the state, does not provide a satisfactory response to these questions in the African context. Therefore, this chapter will attempt to develop guidelines for the economic role of the state by focusing on the specific characteristics of the political economy in Ghana and other African countries and by then developing more general precepts based on practices across the continent over the last thirty years.

THE EVOLUTION OF THE GHANAIAN STATE APPARATUS

As noted in chapter 2, the Ghanaian state, like many others in Africa, expanded dramatically after independence. A significant portion of this expansion was due to efforts to provide greater services (e.g., health, education) to the population and to flesh out the weak colonial state that Nkrumah, like other African nationalists, had inherited. Part of this expansion was also due to an enormous increase in state-owned enterprises (SOEs). Several important SOEs, notably the Cocoa Marketing Board and the Industrial Development Corporation, had been created during the colonial period. Not until after independence, however, did state enterprises boom. By the early 1960s there were more than one hundred parastatals in Ghana. This boom in state enterprises paralleled the experience of other African countries which, irrespective of ideology, were expanding their parastatals. For instance, the number of SOEs in Tanzania increased from eighty to four hundred while those in other countries including Zambia, Senegal, Mali, Côte d'Ivoire, Mauritania, and Madagascar also experienced tremendous growth.[7]

Because of the political and economic convenience of SOEs, by the early 1980s Ghana had a total of 235 state enterprises of which the government had a majority holding in 181.[8] Incomplete data suggest that, by 1980, Ghana's SOEs may have accounted for approximately 50 percent of the formal labor force, compared to the African average of 19 percent.[9]

7. Jacqueline Dutheil de la Rochère, *L'état de la développement économique de la Côte d'Ivoire* (Paris: Centre d'Étude d'Afrique Noire, 1976), 49–51; Ayité-Fily d'Almeida, "La Privatisation des entreprises publiques en Afrique au sud du Sahara-Première partie," *Le Mois en Afrique*, nos. 245–46 (1986): 56; and John Nellis, *Public Enterprises in Sub-Saharan Africa*, World Bank Discussion Paper no. 1 (Washington, D.C.: World Bank, 1986), 56.

8. W. Adda, "Ghana," in *Privatisation in Developing Countries*, ed. V. V. Ramanadham (London: Routledge, 1989), 305.

9. UNDP and the World Bank, *African Economic and Financial Data* (Washington,

Not surprisingly, because so many SOEs had been created for primarily political reasons, they performed particularly poorly as commercial enterprises. For instance, between 1980 and 1982, the deficits of Ghanaian public enterprises were 0.2–3.3 percent of gross domestic product.[10] In 1982 alone, SOEs received approximately 13 percent of total government expenditure in the form of subsidies, equity contributions, and capital grants; by 1984 this figure had almost doubled to 25 percent of total government expenditures.[11] In the felicitous phrasing of the head of Ghana's State Enterprise Commission, "Public enterprises in Ghana have succeeded to combine public sector inefficiency and stagnation with private sector insensitivity to the public interest."[12]

PRIVATIZATION AS AN ANSWER

Given the fiscal drain the SOEs have caused, it is not surprising that privatization and SOE reform are high on Ghana's economic reform agenda. However, it is crucial to note that the motivation for reform comes not from some kind of fundamental rethinking about the state's role in the economy but because of more immediate fiscal and efficiency concerns. As the PNDC has noted, "A substantial part of Central Government expenditures have included transfers to cover losses of public corporations by way of subventions. . . . To check this enormous drain Government has undertaken a major review of the public sector and intends to reduce the burden on itself of such public corporations by divesting itself, wholly or partly, of some of these corporations."[13] Similarly, the World Bank first began to promote SOE reform because of the drain these companies were placing on governments and because they were not performing their stated function.[14] Contrary to what critics of the World Bank suggest, privatization is not the cutting edge of a grand project to implement a fundamentally different vision of what the state

D.C.: World Bank, 1989), 166; and Peter S. Heller and Alan A. Tait, *Government Employment and Pay: Some International Comparisons,* IMF Occasional Paper no. 24 (Washington, D.C.: International Monetary Fund, 1983), 7.

10. Daniel Swanson and Teferra Wolde-Semait, *Africa's Public Enterprise Sector and Evidence of Reforms,* World Bank Technical Paper no. 95 (Washington, D.C.: World Bank, 1989), 31.

11. Adda, "Ghana," 307.

12. W. Adda, "State-Owned Enterprises," mimeo, May 1989, 2.

13. PNDC, *National Programme for Economic Development* (Accra: Government Printer, 1987), 25.

14. Myrna Alexander, "Africa," in *Privatisation in Developing Countries,* ed. V. V. Ramanadham (London: Routledge, 1989), 325.

should be doing. Rather, it is something of an ad hoc response to the fiscal shortfalls of the African state.

Privatization by itself is not a guide to the appropriate future outline of the African state because privatization is not going to significantly change the economic landscape of Ghana or the rest of Africa in the short or medium term. First, because of the anti–private sector policies that successive Ghanaian governments followed for twenty years prior to the early 1980s, there are few Ghanaians with the capital and the management skills to acquire significant public enterprises. Of those who have the capital and skills, many are Lebanese, thus politically unacceptable to the government. Further, there is strong sentiment against selling SOEs because of the controversies that resulted when Ghana attempted a limited divestiture in the early 1970s. As the *Daily Graphic* noted,

> Privatisation is a loaded word. It conjures up in some minds, past experiences where state-owned businesses were disposed of cheaply behind closed doors to favoured cronies. It also raises visions of exploitative rich businessmen taking over and kicking helpless workers into the street to face unemployment.[15]

Second, it is doubtful if many of the companies the government most wants to sell are viable. The SOEs the Rawlings government initially singled out for privatization owed millions of dollars in back taxes and contributions to unfunded pension schemes; their physical plants were run down, and many had almost no managerial capacity. In the end, it is likely that many of these companies will have to be shut down and their assets sold for scrap.[16] That privatization in Africa often centers on divestiture of faltering (or defunct) businesses is not surprising given that the impetus for reform is primarily fiscal. In contrast, the United Kingdom and other European countries often attempt to sell off the most viable firms first because privatization in the developed world is often driven by ideology or the practical desire of leaders to remove the state from management-labor conflicts.

Further, the Rawlings government may simply be unwilling to implement the tough measures necessary to make a company ready for privatization. As one official noted,

> Government companies are grossly overstaffed. We need thinner, leaner kinds of structures. However, where do we put the staff? We are constrained by

15. Quoted in Ben Ephson, "Ghana's Divestiture," *West Africa*, 27 June 1988, 1152.
16. Interview, Accra, 13 August 1990.

government social policy. We do not want to embarrass the government by
putting people on the street. There is a conflict between economic and social
goals.[17]

Clearly, it would be even more difficult for a democratic successor
government that had to devote more attention to popular sensibilities to
implement the drastic reforms necessary to make state-owned corporations attractive to the public. Thus, even with privatization, the number
of people employed by SOEs, as a percentage of the labor market, is
expected to increase.[18] Indeed, the World Bank's structural adjustment
credit required that the PNDC put up only five SOEs for sale and initiate
the sale of five inactive state firms.[19] The rhetoric of privatization and
market forces should not be allowed to obscure the reality of state-
owned enterprises in Ghana and other African countries: these companies are barely functioning in the state sector, and their privatization
will be a tortuous affair that will not significantly alter the economic
landscape.[20]

The surest sign that the privatization movement is not, by itself, an
indication of where the state should end is the fact that most of the effort
going into reforms of state-owned enterprises is to upgrade these companies rather than to sell them off. In Ghana, far more money and effort,
though not publicity, have been spent on reforming such vital state
enterprises as the electrical utility than have been devoted to all the
efforts to privatize. Such an approach makes sense given that 89 percent
of the total losses posted by SOEs in 1986 came from core enterprises
that the government will not sell. Only 7 percent came from SOEs that
are to be divested immediately.[21] More generally, across Africa, the
World Bank has placed more emphasis on reforming state enterprises
than on privatizing them.[22] Privatization then, while a partial answer to
the fiscal problems of the African state, should not be seen as a cure for
all the ills of the state.

17. Interview, Accra, 27 July 1989.
18. J. E. Austin Associates, *MAPS: Country Reference Binder, Summary Report* (Accra: J. E. Austin Associates, 1989), n.p.
19. Peter Nicholas, *The World Bank's Lending for Adjustment,* World Bank Discussion
Paper no. 34 (Washington, D.C.: World Bank, 1988), 53.
20. Many of the same problems affect privatization efforts in other countries with the
result that divestiture can have only a limited effect. See Jeffrey Herbst, "Power and
Privatization in Africa," in *Privatization,* ed. John Waterbury and Ezra Sulieman (Boulder:
Westview, 1990).
21. Austin Associates, *MAPS,* n.p.
22. Don Babai, "The World Bank and the IMF: Rolling Back the State or Backing Its
Role?" in *The Promise of Privatization,* ed. Raymond Vernon (New York: Council on
Foreign Relations, 1988), 266.

THE VISION OF THE STATE UNDER STRUCTURAL ADJUSTMENT

If privatization per se does not suggest where the economic frontiers of the state should be, it may be that a vision of what the state should do has been developed elsewhere in the debate over economic reform. However, for the PNDC, the answer is clear: there is no real view of how to demarcate the economic frontiers of the state. Rather, there is simply the belief that the state should generally contract. PNDC member Justice D. F. Annan is not unusual in arguing that the state must shrink:

> We see now that the policies of state intervention have not worked out as well as we had wanted them to work out. So we are reviewing the entire parastatal sector to see how we can make it more efficient and also scale-down the level of government involvement in industry and commerce.[23]

In the PNDC's relatively few planning documents, there is no mention at all of what the state should actually do in the long term.

The failure of the PNDC to develop a comprehensive vision of the economic role of the state is hardly surprising. Few states have such a coherent vision. It would, for instance, be difficult to outline in detail the U.S. government's vision of the economic role of the state. In addition, the PNDC operates in a mode of continual crisis; its few skilled people do not have the time to think about long-term philosophical issues. When I asked a senior Ministry of Finance official where Ghana would be in five years, he said it was impossible to look at long-term questions: "Right now we are too busy averting disasters. We are only firefighters."[24] It is unlikely that any successor government—which would suffer from the same combination of analytic deficiencies and continual emergencies—would be able to develop a more comprehensive vision in the short to medium term.

In contrast to the PNDC, the World Bank might be expected to have developed a more comprehensive view of the future evolution of the state. However, the World Bank's general writings on the role of the state in Third World countries during economic reform have been remarkably vague. For instance, in the 1983 *World Development Report,* which focused on "management in development," the World Bank tried to outline its conception of the proper role of the state. Unfortunately, the result is not much more instructive than an introductory economics text:

23. Quoted in Achim Rande, "Traditional Values," *West Africa,* 10 March 1986, 507–8.

24. Interview, Accra, 19 July 1989.

Markets may not perform perfectly because of insufficient information or because they do not take adequate account of indirect losses and benefits (the so-called externalities such as pollution or worker training). Nor can free markets handle public goods (such as national defense), where the cost of supply is independent of the number of beneficiaries, or natural monopolies. Finally, markets do not act to correct inequalities in income wealth. Some market failures are so evident that they cannot be ignored; in addition, governments will always have legitimate noneconomic objectives that can be pursued only by intervention.[25]

This kind of statement means little in Africa where market failure is relatively common, information does not flow well, and there are many structural bottlenecks. Nor does this view take into account the fact that public failure may be so great when the state tries to address market failure that it may just be better if the state did not interfere at all. Indeed, all the World Bank seems to suggest is that the trajectory of state growth should be negative; it does not express any vision of a desirable economic role for the state.

In most of its publications on Africa, the World Bank is even more vague as to what the role of the state should be. For instance, the bank's influential report, *Accelerated Development in Sub-Saharan Africa*, presents cogent criticisms of many states' interventions in the economy but does not even begin to outline what the role of the state should be.[26] Similarly, the 1984 report *Toward Sustained Development in Sub-Saharan Africa* claimed only that

> the need for flexibility and adaptability is the single most important lesson of experience. Economic institutions should be responsive to fast-changing circumstances: prescriptions and policy signals need to be assessed, analyzed, and internalized in the country's decision-making process.[27]

Also, the 1986 report *Financing Adjustment with Growth in Sub-Saharan Africa* noted with approval that the size of the state across Africa was shrinking but coupled that approval with the somewhat paradoxical warning that cuts in government spending have led to excessive reductions in equipment, maintenance, operating funds, and materials.[28] The joint report by the United Nations Development Programme

25. World Bank, *World Development Report 1983* (Washington, D.C.: World Bank, 1983), 52.
26. World Bank, *Accelerated Development in Sub-Saharan Africa* (Washington, D.C.: World Bank, 1981).
27. World Bank, *Toward Sustained Development in Sub-Saharan Africa* (Washington, D.C.: World Bank, 1984), 39.
28. World Bank, *Financing Adjustment with Growth in Sub-Saharan Africa, 1986–1990* (Washington, D.C.: World Bank, 1986), 22.

and the World Bank also does not comment on what the actual role of the state should be in Africa.[29] Even the latter's long-term-perspective study on Africa could do little more than approvingly quote Senegal's President Abdou Diouf that "Africa requires not just less government but better government."[30]

Nor does the World Bank develop a fuller picture of what the state should look like during a process of long-term structural adjustment in its specific country reports. For instance, in its report on Ghana, the World Bank does not describe its vision of the future state at all except to list what liberalization entails:

> removing controls and regulation in factor, commodity and foreign exchange markets; de-regulating domestic commodity markets; reducing tariff and non-tariff barriers; elimination of price controls, non-price allocation of credit, interest rate ceilings; and reducing restrictions on financial intermedia-tion.[31]

Similarly, in its report on Guinea-Bissau, the World Bank says nothing about the future of the state except that because of the large public sector deficit, the government should reduce expenditures (in real terms) and endeavor to price all services according to cost.[32] At no point does the report detail what the limits of state intervention in the market should be and thereby establish at least the parameters of the state's economic frontiers.

There are several reasons for the World Bank's inability to express a view on where the state should end. First, an organization composed almost entirely of economists does not have a comparative advantage in the design of political institutions. Second, given the amount of political controversy that almost inevitably accompanies its programs, it is hardly surprising that the World Bank does not want to enter another contentious area. Finally, given its emphasis on project development and medium-term structural development, it is probably incapable as an organization of developing a consensus on where the frontiers of the state should end in Africa. Its failure in this area is an indication of how difficult it is to develop general precepts for reform beyond "getting prices right."

29. United Nations Development Program and World Bank, *Africa's Adjustment and Growth in the 1980's* (Washington, D.C.: World Bank, 1989).

30. World Bank, *Sub-Saharan Africa: From Crisis to Sustainable Growth* (Washington, D.C.: World Bank, 1989), 55.

31. World Bank, *Ghana: Policies and Program for Adjustment* (Washington, D.C.: World Bank, 1984), 68.

32. World Bank, *Guinea-Bissau: A Prescription for Comprehensive Adjustment* (Washington, D.C.: World Bank, 1987), 14.

MARKET AND PUBLIC FAILURES

It has long been recognized that certain market failures require government intervention: externalities and public goods, increasing returns
(which lead to natural monopolies), market imperfections (e.g., too high
transaction costs), and, at a normative level, distributional inequality.[33]
In most economists' view and in the previous quote from the World
Bank, resolving these market failures provides at least something of an
outline for the economic frontiers of the state. The problem with looking
simply at market failure, however, is that the often large costs associated
with state attempts to resolve market failures may outweigh the cost of
the market performing suboptimally. This is especially true in Africa
where governments in countries like Ghana have persuasively demonstrated just how costly government intervention in the economy can be.
As Clive Crook cogently notes, "The question is whether to rely on
imperfect markets or imperfect governments."[34]

It is therefore necessary to consider public failures in addition to the
more conventional private failures when designing the frontiers of the
state. Public failures occur for the same reason that private failures do:
those providing a good face incentives that lead to outcomes divergent
from what is socially desirable.[35]

In general, there are four major types of failure when states try to
solve market failures. First, public agencies may deliver goods at a unit
price higher than is socially desirable because of internal drives to increase budgets, reward certain constituencies by employing more workers than needed, or retain control of information that has very little to do
with providing a service to the public. In Ghana, for instance, SOEs have
not performed well in part because they have been diverted from their
primary commercial purpose to provide jobs for those close to the
leadership and resources (especially revenue from the sale of cocoa) to
public officials.

Second, public agencies may misallocate goods they do produce to
appease certain constituencies. For instance, food and fuel in Ghana, and
many other African countries, have been subsidized to keep the politically important urban population quiescent. Third, public provision of
services may be exceptionally costly because there is no competitive
alternative to the state. Many Ghanaian SOEs provided sub-par services

33. Charles Wolf, "A Theory of Nonmarket Failure: Framework for Implementation
Analysis," *Journal of Law and Economics* 22 (April 1979): 138.
34. Clive Crook, "Survey: The Third World," *Economist,* 23 September 1989, 56.
35. The next three paragraphs are based partially on Wolf, "Nonmarket Failure," 112.

or goods; but there was often nothing to judge these products against, and consumers had no choice but to buy them. Finally, government actions may increase the inequity of the power distribution by giving bureaucrats, military officials, or whoever else enforces state regulations greater authority and opportunities to become richer by demanding side payments from those who want access to government-regulated goods or services.[36] For instance, as noted in chapter 3, foreign exchange licensing in Ghana allowed public officials to collect enormous rents from those who needed imported inputs to run their factories.

In Ghana and the rest of Africa, public failures have been especially notable for several reasons. African administrative structures have always been exceptionally weak, and these limitations have been compounded by other aspects of public administration that provided high incentives for government officials to act in socially undesirable ways. For instance, governments in Ghana and elsewhere have been unable to erect any kind of barrier between politicians and the managers who operated SOEs. Therefore, there is a continual temptation for politicians to use SOEs to their own benefit or that of the constituencies they serve. Also, few African governments have developed electoral systems whereby poorly functioning politicians can be removed from office, so there was little reason for those who oversaw public enterprises to behave in socially desirable ways. Instead, many African governments have devolved into elaborate patrimonial systems where the control of parastatal resources is politically important to national leaders.

The question then becomes how to weigh market versus public failure when exploring how the economic frontiers of the African state should be determined. Unfortunately, public choice analysis, after persuasively analyzing the reasons for market and public failure, is not generally up to the task of analyzing when one type of failure will be greater than the other. For instance, Wolf argues that while the question of whether externalities generated by firms or unduly costly provision of services by governments is greater is an "analytically interesting, and operationally crucial, question . . . the answer is, in general, indeterminate."[37] At least part of the problem, as Robert Bates notes, is that political outcomes

36. Ibid., 116–28. See also Joseph E. Stiglitz, *The Economic Role of the State* (Oxford: Basil Blackwell, 1989), 45.

37. Wolf, "Nonmarket Failure," 117. Nor is Wolf able to develop the argument further in his later book, *Markets or Governments: Choosing Between Imperfect Alternatives* (Cambridge, Mass.: MIT Press, 1988). See also Dieter Helm, "The Economic Borders of the State," in *The Economic Borders of the State*, ed. Dieter Helm (Oxford: Oxford University Press, 1989), 20–21.

cannot be analyzed by simply transferring the tools economists have developed to understand the workings of governments.[38]

There is some agreement that the state in Africa has to be involved in many functions traditionally reserved to the state across the world: national defense, provision of education, provision of infrastructure. Because these goods must be provided on a large scale, the government is at no disadvantage compared to the private sector.[39] In addition, the public goods problem makes it unlikely that many of these services will be offered by the private sector. This is not to say how much of any one of these services the state should provide or who should be the final supplier of these goods (e.g., public schools or mission schools), just that it is clear that the state will play a leading role in deciding how these goods should be produced and consumed. However, there is still a large gray area concerning what the state should do in addition to providing those goods, like national defense, that have traditionally been seen as a function of the public sector. In other words, what should be the economic frontiers of the state in Africa?

By explicitly taking account of the particular features of the political economies of African countries, it may be possible to step into the breach caused by public choice's inability to take the market/nonmarket comparison beyond the level of high theory. These features are best understood by developing a series of "stylized facts" about the state and the economy in Africa.

In Ghana and most other African countries there is

an absolute shortage of trained manpower and administrative expertise in both the private and public sectors;

an economy characterized by extremely high transaction costs because infrastructure (including roads, ports, railroads) is not extensive and in many places is crumbling, statistical services are rudimentary at best, and communications lines are poor;

a governmental structure where there can be no guarantee that SOEs will be allowed to respond to price signals without political interference;

a government that does not look to the private sector for political support. Correspondingly, some of the best capitalized and most capable

38. Robert H. Bates, "A Critique by Political Scientists," in *Politics and Policy Making in Developing Countries,* ed. Gerald M. Meier (San Francisco: International Center for Economic Growth, 1991), 264.

39. Anne O. Krueger, *Government Failures in Development,* NBER Working Paper no. 3340 (Cambridge, Mass.: National Bureau of Economic Research, 1990), 13.

entrepreneurs are viewed with suspicion by government and sometimes actively discriminated against because of their size (multinational corporations), their former citizenship (e.g., Lebanese in Ghana and elsewhere in West Africa, Indians in East Africa), their ethnic group, or simply because they are successful;

capital markets that are weak, if they function at all. There is usually no futures market, that is, a market for risk bearing in conditions of uncertainty.[40]

Taking account of these factors makes the analysis much more realistic. This approach is therefore far more persuasive than those that "assume away the influence of ideological, historical, and political factors" when trying to understand the economic boundaries of the state.[41]

ENHANCING THE MARKET

A first clear role of the state in Ghana and the rest of Africa is to reduce the transaction costs and bottlenecks in their economies. Indeed, it is one of the paradoxes in Africa that an activist state is needed to promote market forces. In Ghana this has meant the rehabilitation, reconstruction, and construction of the road, phone, and electrical networks. Indeed, the World Bank since 1983 has concentrated on road reconstruction as a crucial area because even the most rudimentary economic activity, such as shipping cocoa to the ports, will not be profitable if poor roads cause transport costs to be too high. Since the government must assume responsibility for these infrastructure improvements, there will be a noticeable increase in resources flowing to the state for a long time. For instance, despite the fact that since 1983 the World Bank has devoted a significant amount of money to Ghanaian road construction, not until the late 1990s will Ghanaian roads be back to the condition they were at independence in 1957.

In addition, the state must ensure property rights if there is to be development. Douglass C. North and Robert Paul Thomas, in their economic history of Europe, eloquently suggest the importance of property rights: "Economic growth will occur if property rights make it

40. Heinz W. Arndt, " 'Market Failure' and Underdevelopment," *World Development* 16 (February 1988): 225.

41. Leroy P. Jones and Edward S. Mason, "Why Public Enterprises?" in *Public Enterprises in Less-Developed Countries,* ed. Leroy P. Jones (Cambridge: Cambridge University Press, 1982), 24.

worthwhile to undertake socially productive activity."[42] Unfortunately, few African governments have understood the importance of property rights. Indeed, the first Rawlings government's destruction of markets in 1979 and the PNDC's seizure of property and public beatings of market-women in 1982 in efforts to enforce price controls created a great deal of uncertainty concerning the role of property rights in Ghana. Indeed, there are anecdotal reports in Ghana of marketwomen converting each day's earnings into dollars because they still do not trust the government after it revoked 50-cedi notes in 1982. The Rawlings regime now regrets these measures, but they linger in public memory, creating a credibility problem for the government (this problem also affects many other African countries, though probably not to the same degree). Clearly, the regime and successor governments must take efforts to ensure that the law and property rights are respected in the future.

African governments must also develop other important economic institutions necessary for the development of capital markets and the promotion of general economic growth. For instance, the Rawlings regime's promotion of the stock market, which opened in December 1990, is a very important step in aiding market forces. Independent of its actual economic effect, institutional creation of the type exemplified by the stock market sends an important signal to investors that the government is trying to strengthen the institutions of the private sector. Indeed, that the once populist PNDC is sponsoring a stock market is an especially important sign to all actors in the economy that the government views structural adjustment as irreversible. Correspondingly, if there is to develop a constituency for structural adjustment, institutions such as the stock market will be an important pole around which proreform constituencies can coalesce. Thus, to simply look at the stock market's capitalization in the years immediately following its creation is to miss the importance of new economic institutions that will offer long-term economic and political support for the policies the PNDC has adopted.

Another clear area where the state will have to be involved in Ghana and the rest of Africa is natural monopolies—for example, electrical generation and telephones. In theory, the state can either own natural monopolies outright or allow them to be privately owned but regulate them so they do not exploit their monopoly position. Given that administrative expertise in Africa is so limited, it probably makes sense that the

42. Douglass C. North and Robert Paul Thomas, *The Rise of the Western World* (Cambridge: Cambridge University Press, 1973), 8.

government should run these monopolies because the creation of a separate regulatory system requiring many trained administrators would simply impose more demands on the African state where it is weakest. Of course, publicly owned monopolies in Africa can still be highly inefficient, as they can be in the private sector, but at least the public ownership of monopolies eliminates a potentially draining regulatory bureaucracy.

ROLE OF STATE-OWNED CORPORATIONS

In addition to these basic areas, the state may have another important economic role to play. Sir W. Arthur Lewis, who preferred that industrialization be left to foreign and domestic capitalists, did argue that state ownership could play an important role in "pioneering" industries. He suggested that, given entrepreneurs' lack of experience, the state should take the lead in industries it thought would succeed and then sell the industries back to the private sector once they had been successfully established.[43] This argument immediately runs into the same problem that many other justifications for state involvement do: there is no reason to believe that the state has an advantage in being able to perceive which industries will be successful. The historical record also suggests that African countries are particularly ill-suited to develop SOEs that could become immediately viable as private enterprises.

However, Lewis and others who note that the state will have to adopt some kind of interventionist role in the economy because of the private sector's deficiencies are, in general, correct. This is especially true since foreign capital, which Lewis suggested would play the crucial role in promoting industrialization, currently shows little interest in Ghana or the rest of Africa. In addition, economic theory suggests that there is nothing wrong with state ownership as long as firms are allowed to respond to prices and follow commercial considerations. Economists have usually ended their discussion of the economic role of the state at this point, but, given the stylized facts developed above, the analysis can be furthered by asking the simple question, Under what circumstances is an SOE most likely to be allowed to operate as a commercial concern?

State-owned corporations will operate most like commercial firms when there is a strong institutional barrier between the SOE and officials

43. W. Arthur Lewis, *Report on Industrialization and the Gold Coast* (Accra: Government Printer, 1953), 21.

who would manipulate the firms for political reasons.[44] If SOE managers are insulated from noncommercial considerations, they have a good chance to operate as a "normal" commercial firm. However, it is unlikely that this kind of institutional separatism can be guaranteed in Ghana or many other African countries. The PNDC operates without a constitution, as do most military governments in Africa, and the kind of institutional guarantees that a commercial SOE would need are therefore often lacking. The various institutional fixes (e.g., parastatal commissions, requiring the SOEs to report directly to the president) that many African governments have used to try to promote parastatal distinctiveness have usually fared poorly.[45]

Since impermeable institutional barriers are not likely in the near future, governments should develop administrative practices that will make it easier to discern if state enterprises are operating on a commercial basis. For instance, public enterprises should not be given an explicit monopoly when prospects exist for competition from the private sector. A competitive environment will force state-owned enterprises to operate on a commercial basis and, just as important, will provide important yardsticks in the form of prices and levels of service with which to measure the performance of the state firms. Of course, the state can still subsidize SOEs, but noncommercial operations in a competitive environment are at least easier to detect and object to. In addition, SOEs that perform poorly are bound to do less damage to the national economy if they do not monopolize a sector of the economy.

There is also a strong argument that SOEs are more likely to be successful when they are forced to operate in an environment where prices are set on the international level. In such a situation, it will also be obvious when noncommercial considerations have become too important. For instance, while the World Bank has, in general, criticized the performance of many African SOEs, it did note that mineral exporting parastatals and some SOEs trading in export crops have performed notably better than other African state corporations.[46] Obviously, one of the reasons for the relative success of these parastatals is that there is a clear yardstick in the form of international prices against which to

44. Armeane M. Choksi, *State Intervention in the Industrialization of Developing Countries: Selected Issues,* World Bank Staff Working Paper no. 341 (Washington, D.C.: World Bank, 1979), 69.

45. See, for instance, Jeffrey Herbst, "Political Impediments to Economic Rationality: Why Zimbabwe Cannot Reform Its Public Sector," *Journal of Modern African Studies* 27, no. 1 (1989).

46. World Bank, *Accelerated Development,* 38.

measure their performance. For instance, it is easy for farmers, the government, and aid donors concerned with reform to develop good measures of the efficiency of marketing parastatals just by calculating the percentage of the world price received by farmers. It is much harder to calculate how parastatals are treating farmers who produce food for internal consumption.[47]

International price standards do not guarantee that SOEs will not perform poorly. Indeed, the Ghanaian cocoa board was a classic example of a disastrous SOE because its consistent taxation of cocoa farmers eventually led to Ghana's losing a substantial portion of its share of the world cocoa market. However, in contrast to many other Ghanaian SOEs—whose operations, although also deficient, were outside the public's view—at least it was clear to everyone just how the cocoa board was malfunctioning and whom it was hurting. As Elizabeth Ohene wrote, "The first rung in the long ladder of leeches that feed on the sweat of the cocoa farmers is the Cocoa Marketing Board—it is well known and well documented that one of if not *the* plum organisation in the public service is the CMB."[48] Indeed, Flt. Lt. Rawlings's central indictment against the previous regimes is that they exploited the cocoa farmers to subsidize the rest of the nation.[49] Assuming a relatively well intentioned government, SOEs operating where international prices provide a benchmark can be expected to do well. Indeed, by the late 1980s the cocoa board under the PNDC had made enormous strides and was paying farmers a significantly higher percentage of the world price than it had.[50]

It is also important to note what SOEs are especially poor at. The state should not be involved in commercial operations when such operations stifle private sector activity, when there are no standards by which to judge operations, or when economies of scale are not present (e.g., food retailing, other locally performed services). Indeed, there should be a presumption that the farther a commercial operation gets from the necessity of a large-scale organization where information on performance is readily available, the less likely it is that the state needs to be involved.

47. Thus, the recent World Bank statistical collection on Africa contains useful tables on the percentage of the world price that farmers receive for various crops but very little data on the fate of peasants growing foodstuffs. World Bank, *African Economic and Financial Data* (Washington, D.C.: World Bank, 1989), 146–50.
48. "Words, Deeds & Cocoa," *West Africa*, 31 August 1982, 2104. Emphasis in the original.
49. See chapter 5.
50. World Bank, *African Economic and Financial Data*, 147.

OTHER ECONOMIC ROLES OF THE STATE

It is also possible to sketch out other possible roles for the state. One particular area in which the state has a comparative advantage over the private sector is in mobilizing capital. Capital markets in Ghana and the rest of Africa are underdeveloped, and investors may not be willing to risk their own funds because they fear future changes in government policies or are uncertain about the strength of the economy. In Ghana, despite relatively good economic performance since 1983, investors have been unwilling to invest capital because of uncertainty about the PNDC's future economic policy. However, the state has, in Lindblom's term, "no fingers" when it comes to management because of the many possibilities for public failure enumerated above.[51]

Therefore, although in many cases African states can provide capital for SOEs to begin operations, they should allow management to be firmly in the hands of the private sector. Allowing the private sector to manage state-owned firms would also increase the likelihood that the state firms would be insulated from political decisions and that these companies would be able to respond to price signals. Indeed, in Ghana and the rest of Africa, this kind of reform is much more feasible than privatization precisely because of weak capital markets. State ownership and private sector management would also alleviate the fears of many African governments that actors in the private sector would accumulate too much power if they were to gain outright ownership of too much of what was previously possessed by the state. While management contracts and other measures that "privatize" the operation of state firms are also extremely difficult to implement, they should at least be considered as part of the arsenal of measures used to reform state enterprises. Privatization, a glamorous policy with little application in Africa, has received far too much attention while more useful measures like management contracts have been understudied.

The boundaries of the state can also be defined spatially. State intervention in the economy should be biased in favor of rural projects. Entrepreneurs have a strong incentive to invest in projects in Accra, Tema, or Kumasi right now because, as in most African countries, these are the only areas where infrastructure is relatively well developed. The PNDC has made what is now the customary pledge in Africa to develop infrastructure in the rural areas, but given past performance, entrepre-

51. Charles E. Lindblom, *Politics and Markets: The World's Political-Economic Systems* (New York: Basic Books, 1977), 65.

neurs doubt the government will become truly committed to the rural areas. State intervention is therefore probably most justified in the rural areas. Through such intervention the state will be able to compensate for the private sector's uncertainty over its intentions; further, giving special attention to the rural areas will signal the private sector that greater attention to the countryside is warranted. Correspondingly, there is less reason for the state to be involved in projects in the urban areas where there can be much greater certainty about the future level of economic activity. A bias for state involvement in the rural areas would also have the added advantage of allowing the state to collect more information on the developing rural economy.

WHAT THE STATE SHOULD NOT DO

In defining the economic boundaries of the state, it is important to suggest what the state should not do. In particular, African states should not adopt interventionist policies that curtail the flow of information in their economies. Many of the guidelines developed above are designed to increase the flow of information in African countries, irrespective of who holds actual ownership. If information, especially concerning prices, is allowed to be transmitted with relatively little hindrance, there is a better chance of economic actors both within and without the state making decisions that result in efficient use of resources. Studies of other countries that have been economically successful, notably South Korea, suggest that policymakers within the state were able to make correct decisions because price signals were freely transmitted to them.[52] Indeed, access to price information is one of the outstanding features of many of the fast-growing East Asian economies, which otherwise had large amounts of state intervention. State intervention is not pernicious in East Asia in part because, unlike much of Africa, it does not lead to distortions in price and other information.

Unfortunately, many regulations that Ghana and other African countries adopted were expressly designed to suppress price information and other flows of information. Price controls and fixed exchange rates in particular made it difficult for private firms or SOEs to make proper commercial choices. Indeed, this suppression of information has been a particularly important problem in Ghana because firms' and consumers' ability to ferret out information in the face of distorted prices is limited

52. World Bank, *Korea: Managing the Industrial Transition*, vol. 1 (Washington, D.C.: World Bank, 1987), 35.

by lack of trained manpower, inadequate research facilities, and the organizational decay brought on by the years of economic decline. Thus, government actions that distort prices in African countries are especially pernicious because economic decisionmakers have so few other sources of information on which to rely.

The elimination of price and exchange rate controls in Ghana has allowed prices and other information to flow more freely within the economy with consequent benefits. In fact, Ghanaian policymakers argue that one of the reasons they decided to allow bureaus to trade foreign currencies freely was that they were aware that there was a significant black market, and they wanted to receive the information the illegal market was generating. As one PNDC member noted, "We knew these transactions [illegal trading of foreign currency] were taking place. We wanted these transactions to move from the underground and become transparent."[53] Similarly, an official in the Ministry of Finance suggested that problems in areas such as infrastructure and management became apparent only after distortions in the exchange rate had been eliminated. He argued that it was impossible to begin to solve these problems until policymakers were able to make evaluations using undistorted prices.[54]

AFRICAN STATES AND THE LESSONS OF THE ASIAN COUNTRIES

At one level, the recommendations presented for what the African state should and should not do correspond to many of the lessons learned from the successful countries of East Asia. The suggested frontiers allow market forces to operate and allow information to be transmitted much more easily throughout the economy, as has occurred in South Korea, Taiwan, and other Asian nations.

However, whether African countries can engage in the dramatic state interventions to develop certain sectors or industries as East Asian countries did is unclear. First, the current development challenge facing most African countries is to develop or rehabilitate the basic institutions and infrastructure that will make development possible. Put baldly, most African countries will be fortunate if, by the end of the 1990s, they return to the level of institutional and infrastructure development that they had achieved at independence in the early 1960s. Thus, African countries must first concentrate on establishing the preconditions for

53. Interview, Accra, 10 August 1989.
54. Interview, Accra, 19 July 1989.

development—especially property rights, functioning capital markets, and working infrastructure—before ambitious plans to intervene in specific sectors can be considered.

Second, if the political systems of African countries, especially the constituency base, do not change, ambitious sectoral intervention policies may simply mask a return to the bad old days of market-distorting government policies designed to cultivate political support rather than promote growth. As noted in chapter 1, the fact that most African governments do not look to the private sector for significant political support makes it unlikely that these governments would intervene solely to promote growth. Also, the legacy of failure weighs heavily on African countries. The East Asian countries conducted their significant sectoral interventions with no history of states intervening primarily for political reasons irrespective of the economic damage caused. However, in African countries, where state intervention is almost automatically assumed to be linked to the political needs of leaders, sectoral intervention may be much less credible and will always be prone to capture by the political calculations of leaders. Of course, if growth were to occur, constituencies might develop in the private sector that would make the possibility of the state's intervening specifically to help private sector growth more likely. However, until African governments undergo such a metamorphosis, they are probably better off focusing solely on the important tasks of establishing the preconditions for development.

SIZE OF THE STATE

Much of the debate that has occurred concerning the economic role of the state has centered on the size of the state. The World Bank has, at least obliquely, suggested that the state is too large in Africa and should be scaled back. Some have described current efforts by international donors and bankers as "taking the state back out" of economic policy.[55] The Ghanaian rhetoric on state reform also suggests that the primary emphasis in reforming the state should be on reducing its size. Others, reacting to the World Bank's rhetoric, have criticized suggestions that the size of the state should be reduced.[56]

55. Michael Bratton, "Beyond the State: Civil and Associational Life in Africa," *World Politics* 41, no. 4 (April 1989): 408.
56. See, for instance, Economic Commission for Africa, *African Alternative Framework to Structural Adjustment Programmes for Socio-Economic Recovery and Transformation* (Addis Ababa: Economic Commission for Africa, 1989).

However, the analysis developed above suggests that the size of the state, usually measured as public spending as a percentage of gross domestic product, is not by itself a particularly interesting consideration. What is important is that the state perform the functions it can do best and withdraw from those wherein analysis suggests it is doing too much damage. There is some evidence that, at least in countries that have become as impoverished as Ghana, if the economy is to grow, the state will have to expand to fulfill the tasks it must accomplish. First, because of the long period of economic decline, Ghana and many other African countries have faced a protracted fiscal crisis which has caused their state to contract. State institutions that collect statistics, maintain infrastructure, and help govern the economy have often atrophied to dangerous levels. Indeed, as in Ghana in the early 1980s, sometimes the state has simply run out of money to accomplish the basic tasks needed for markets to run smoothly. Thus, economic recovery will almost automatically mean some increase in state size.

Second, just the extraordinary expenses that will have to be incurred to (re)construct the infrastructure will require significant state expansion. For instance, in part because of external capital flows to aid infrastructure, government expenditures as a percentage of gross domestic product in Ghana increased from a low of 8.25 percent in 1983 to 14.17 percent in 1988.[57] It is likely that the state will, with the help of multilateral organizations, have to spend even more in the future if the infrastructure is to be developed to a level at which transaction costs can be substantially reduced.

Understanding the proper economic frontiers is therefore not a question of necessarily "rolling back the state" but redistributing state activities so that the state does what only it can do and leaves the rest to the private sector. If the state is larger after this redistribution, it should not matter. This perspective is important because some have confused the absolute size of the state with criticisms of how the state functions.[58] Countries such as Kenya, which throughout the 1980s had states twice as large as Ghana's, are not necessarily more "statist." That is, simply because the state was larger in Kenya did not mean that it was more economically counterproductive than Ghana's had been. Paradoxically, states such as Kenya may be less "statist" than Ghana if state size and

57. International Monetary Fund, *Government Finance Statistics Yearbook* (Washington, D.C.: IMF, 1990), p. 94.
58. See, for instance, Lynn Krieger Mytelka, "The Unfulfilled Promise of African Industrialization," *African Studies Review* 32, no. 3 (December 1989): 98.

power are used to promote economic activity in ways that only the state can rather than to interfere with legitimate private sector activity. It is how that money is spent, along with how the government regulates the economy, that determines if government is helping or hindering private economic activity.

CONCLUSION

Centering the debate concerning the economic frontiers of the state on important substantive issues such as the flow of information is more constructive than adhering to the ideological precepts of socialists or free-marketeers. The African reality differs too radically from the assumptions of properly working governments or economies for the application of general theories to be fruitful. Ironically, economic and public choice theories, which their proponents claim are opposed to the ideologically driven rhetoric of socialists or free-marketeers, are also unable to make a substantive contribution to the demarcation of the African state because these theories, too, are incapable of taking into account African realities. Only an eclectic mix of guidelines grounded in the realities of how the economy and the state actually work in Ghana and the rest of Africa will usefully suggest what the state should do for whom.

CHAPTER 7

Ghana, the Multilateral Organizations, and the International Economy

The actions of the IMF and the World Bank will always be central to the politics of structural adjustment in Africa. Indeed, the involvement of the multilaterals in what had previously been considered the sovereign domestic policy decisions of African countries was one of the most important and most controversial developments in the Third World during the 1980s. Given that the World Bank and the IMF will probably continue to expand their role during the 1990s, it is particularly important to understand the interaction between international aid organizations and African governments. Since the PNDC government has had one of the longest sustained relationships with the multilaterals in Africa, the Ghanaian case is especially important in this regard.

After reviewing the history of Ghana's relationship with the World Bank and the IMF in the 1980s, this chapter will analyze the political dynamics of conditionality and the timing of reforms. These exceptionally important issues have often been debated only by assertion in the economic literature because the political relationships between the multilaterals and African governments have been underanalyzed. The chapter will then analyze how reforms recommended by the World Bank and the IMF will affect Ghana's relationship with the international economy and, eventually, with the multilaterals themselves. Thus this chapter, which examines the interaction between Ghana and the international economy, is the analogue to chapter 6, which examined the domestic economic frontiers of the state.

GHANA AND THE MULTILATERALS

The Economic Recovery Programme that the Ghanaians finally launched in 1983 was technically a home-grown plan. However, the constant interaction among the IMF, the World Bank, and Ghanaian civil servants over the years inevitably meant that the PNDC's program had been heavily influenced by the thinking of the multilaterals. In addition, the immediate problems that Ghana faced in 1983 were so stark and so obvious that there was no way that any serious reform effort could avoid the problems of devaluation, pricing, and deficit reduction, issues of central concern to the World Bank and IMF.

In the early years of the ERP, especially between 1983 and 1986, the IMF took the lead in providing external finance for the ERP.[1] Of the $1 billion in additional external assistance provided to the PNDC up to 1986, 60 percent came from the IMF. In contrast, the World Bank provided only 14 percent of the additional inflows. The IMF took such a prominent position because the early goals of the ERP centered on increasing exports, eliminating or reducing the extraordinary macroeconomic imbalances that had developed, and reestablishing Ghana's international creditworthiness. The IMF, as the provider of the international "Good Housekeeping seal of approval," was the obvious agency to help Ghana.

After 1986, the comparative advantage of the IMF in helping Ghana diminished while that of the World Bank increased. Three years into the recovery program the government had made substantial progress on some of the major macroeconomic imbalances and was increasingly turning its attention to rehabilitation of infrastructure, pricing decisions, and sectoral rehabilitation. Naturally, the World Bank would take the lead in all these areas. Also, the high interest rates on the money the IMF loaned to Ghana was beginning to create a debt-servicing problem. As table 3 indicates, while Ghana did receive large new inflows of aid, much of that money immediately left the country again to service old debts or to repay the IMF. The World Bank's terms were much easier, and increasing reliance on the bank has been one of the reasons for the jump in net inflows of aid to Ghana as the ERP progressed.

By the late 1980s and continuing into the early 1990s, the World Bank

---

1. I rely here on John Toye, "Ghana," in *Aid and Power*, vol. 2, ed. Paul Mosley, Jane Harrigan, and John Toye (New York: Routledge, 1991), 159–63.

TABLE 3   ACTUAL AND PROJECTED AID FLOWS
(millions of U.S. $)

	1983	1984	1985	1986	1987	1988	1989	1990	1991
Capital Inflows									
ODA	110	258	224	358	437	499	569	629	622
Medium-term debt	114	170	153	133	109	118	56	51	35
IMF	340	218	124	38	149	210	188	131	62
Payments									
Debt	125	115	248	251	182	208	184	123	122
Interest	82	101	106	105	126	142	115	106	105
IMF	16	4	0	22	174	255	184	111	66
Arrears	0	208	57	4	71	30	45	25	0
Net Position	341	218	90	147	142	192	285	446	426

SOURCES: World Bank, *African Economic and Financial Data* (Washington, D.C.: World Bank, 1989); Ghana, *Towards a New Dynamism: Report Prepared by the Government of Ghana for the Fifth Meeting of the Consultative Group for Ghana* (Accra: Government Printer, 1989), 30; and private communication from the Ministry of Finance.

NOTE: There is some disagreement between the sources concerning the actual level of disbursements in 1983.

had come to take the dominant position, not only vis-à-vis the IMF, but also in regard to all other donors in Ghana. The bank's sectoral loans in particular came to be extremely prominent. The IMF's role was accordingly reduced to monitoring the exchange rate and other macroeconomic variables. The IMF did allow Ghana access to progressively cheaper money through the Extended Fund Facility and the Structural Adjustment Facility. In 1988, these relatively generous facilities were replaced by an Extended Structural Adjustment Facility, an even less restrictive IMF loan to which only a few countries in Africa enjoyed access.

Ghana's relationship with the multilaterals appears to be a success. Indeed, the study by Mosley, Harrigan, and Toye notes that Ghana actually implemented most of the agreed-upon conditions in the order they were proposed, a rare event in the study's sample of countries.[2] Martin also notes the "astonishing degree of compliance" that Ghana

2. Paul Mosley, Jane Harrigan, and John Toye, *Aid and Power*, vol. 1: *The World Bank and Policy-Based Lending* (New York: Routledge, 1991), 114.

had with World Bank and IMF conditions during the 1983–1989 period.[3] Ghana authorities, although they have had their disagreements with the multilaterals, some of which are detailed below, seem generally pleased with the relationship with the World Bank and the IMF.

Still, the actions taken in Ghana by the IMF and the World Bank are controversial: many have criticized the approaches of the multilaterals. These criticisms may not be completely fair to the Ghanaian experience because they are based on what we have learned since the imposition of the Economic Recovery Programme and therefore enjoy the benefit of hindsight. Still, examining these criticisms is important because they may suggest important lessons for other countries that want to implement elements of Ghana's ERP program. Also, examining these criticisms is necessary given the lack of any persuasive alternative to current reform proposals and because the World Bank's analytical framework still needs to be developed.[4]

STRICTNESS OF CONDITIONALITY

A major criticism of orthodox reform programs has been that the International Monetary Fund in particular has been too demanding in its conditionality. As former president of Tanzania Julius Nyerere said, "When did the IMF become an International Ministry of Finance? When did nations agree to surrender to it their power of decision making?"[5] Similarly, a major review of adjustment by a group of experts argued that the IMF's conditionality has become too tight and that too many conditions are imposed on countries. For instance, it noted that nearly 80 percent of the IMF arrangements between 1983 and 1985 contained, on average, eight performance criteria.[6] This issue is particularly difficult because, given the political logic of poor economic policies, without strict conditionality politicians may not have enough incentive to make the difficult reforms that structural adjustment demands.

However, countries may differ from the IMF on legitimate issues

3. Matthew Martin, "Negotiating Adjustment and External Finance: Ghana and the International Community, 1982–1989," in *Ghana: The Political Economy of Reform,* ed. Donald Rothchild (Boulder: Lynne Rienner, 1991), 240.

4. See Fahrettin Yagci, Steven Kamin, and Vicki Rosenbaum, *Structural Adjustment Lending: An Evaluation of Program Design,* World Bank Staff Working Paper no. 735 (Washington, D.C.: World Bank, 1985), 1–2.

5. Quoted in John Loxley, "Alternative Approaches to Stabilization in Africa," in *Africa and the International Monetary Fund,* ed. Gerald K. Helleiner (Washington, D.C.: IMF, 1986), 119.

6. The Group of 24 report is reprinted in *IMF Survey,* 10 August 1987, 8.

including political calculations, desired income distribution, and the eventual design of their economy, and such differences might make strict IMF conditionality difficult to justify or implement.[7] Indeed, strict conditionality is not inherent in IMF programs. The IMF had looser requirements in the 1970s, and its legislative history suggests that when the organization was founded there was considerable sentiment that it not interfere in the sovereign decisions of nations.[8] The IMF admits that much of its current operating procedure is based on little more than the "oral tradition" passed down by generations of officials.[9] An analytic perspective on the strictness of conditionality is therefore desperately needed.

The question of strict IMF conditionality became a central issue in Ghana between 1983 and 1986. Despite the fact that after 1983 Ghana fulfilled every IMF target, the fund continued to insist on extremely strict measures regarding the budget deficit, money supply, and exchange rate. Indeed, when the ERP began to slip in 1986, the IMF suspended its standby program, and the World Bank delayed its disbursement of program loans for ninety days.[10] This hurt the credibility of proadjustment PNDC officials and made the program that much more difficult to implement. Ghanaian officials expressed considerable bitterness that the IMF did not trust them more after three years of implementing extremely difficult programs. Strict conditionality can help proadjustment officials argue their case by making it clear that the IMF will not negotiate. However, conditionality in Ghana's case seems to have gone beyond the point where it was politically beneficial to proadjustment officials.

The Ghanaian experience and similar complaints from almost every other country that has had dealings with the IMF and the World Bank have caused many to suggest that the nature of conditionality should be changed. For instance, John Loxley has argued that standby programs should be front-loaded so that countries receive most of the funds from the IMF before they introduce their reform program or soon after. This would have the effect of reducing IMF leverage and increasing the political maneuverability of African governments.[11] Similarly, Martin

7. Some of these points are stressed by Loxley, "Alternative Approaches," 127.
8. Sidney Dell, *On Being Grandmotherly: The Evolution of IMF Conditionality,* Essays in International Finance no. 144 (Princeton: International Finance Section, 1981), 1–10.
9. International Monetary Fund, *Theoretical Aspects of the Design of Fund-Supported Adjustment Programs,* IMF Occasional Paper no. 55 (Washington, D.C.: IMF, 1987), 1.
10. Martin, "Negotiating Adjustment," 249.
11. Loxley, "Alternative Approaches," 134.

argues that the IMF and the World Bank must show more flexibility than they have done if other countries are going to successfully implement the reforms.[12]

However, there are still strong arguments for strict conditionality. Most important, in the early years it was uncertain if the IMF and World Bank could trust the PNDC to implement the reforms, given the notable failures of previous governments and the Rawlings government's own early history. As Deepak Lal notes, the lack of credibility inevitably affects the degree of conditionality:

> If in the past a government has reversed preannounced plans because the costs of reversal (say, increased inflation) seemed to be lower than the benefits (say, financing a public sector deficit), then an announced adjustment program which is reversible may be unsustainable. Even if the "new" government has in fact changed its character, before outside creditors are willing to provide capital for smoothing intertemporal consumption, the government may have to demonstrate its newfound resolution by undertaking more Draconian disabsorption measures than would have been required if its announcements were credible.[13]

In hindsight, as Martin suggests, it is clear that the PNDC was serious in its reforms, and therefore strict conditionality should have been loosened. However, this argument does not suggest how the IMF and the World Bank could have known when conducting negotiations, especially early in the recovery program, that the Rawlings government was committed to implementing reforms as opposed to trying simply to muddle through another foreign exchange crisis with the IMF's help. The issue becomes particularly difficult because African countries are well aware of how each other does with the IMF and the World Bank. Therefore, loose IMF conditionality with one country may affect negotiations with a country that may not deserve such a concession.

FOCUSING ON INSTITUTIONAL CHANGE

The question then becomes how uncertainty about government intentions can be reduced so that the IMF can loosen its strict conditionality policy in certain cases without yielding the leverage needed to counteract the political advantages of inadequate policies or setting an unfortunate precedent. The most persuasive response to this challenge would be to

12. Martin, "Negotiating Adjustment," 259.
13. Deepak Lal, "The Political Economy of Economic Liberalization," *World Bank Economic Review* 1 (January 1987): 275.

judge government intentions by reforms in economic institutions rather than by such economic measures as the size of the fiscal deficit, which, after all, can indicate only temporary changes and can be altered. For instance, more than a few countries have met their IMF target for the fiscal deficit simply by not issuing certain checks for a few days.

Changes in real economic institutions, especially the shedding of decision-making power by the state to the market, indicate a degree of commitment to economic reform that should be rewarded by a loosening of conditionality. Reforming economic institutions in this way is particularly important because it makes reversal of policy much more difficult in the future. Governments could, of course, take back authority they had given to the market to set prices on goods or foreign exchange, but this would be a much more difficult and obvious step than, say, letting the fiscal deficit slip beyond the parameters agreed to with the IMF.

A focus on changes in economic institutions is also useful because often it is a good gauge of the factional politics within the leadership revolving around economic reform. Governments can make many policy changes and still be mired in factional disputes that will eventually derail an economic reform program. For instance, a one-time devaluation does not indicate that a government is irrevocably committed to a reform program. Antireform politicians may have simply suffered a temporary setback; as long as the government retains control over the exchange rate it has not lost the ability to return to past exchange rate policies. Thus, in 1986, Lieutenant Colonel Assasie realized that as long as Ghana continued to devalue administratively, there was a chance to derail the recovery program. However, once the auction was adopted and the government lost the ability to determine the exchange rate, it became much more difficult to reverse reforms in this area. Substantively and symbolically, changes in economic institutions are a clear indication that proadjustment forces have consolidated their power and have won outright victories that cannot be rescinded.

Therefore, in operational terms, the importance of institutional change in reducing the uncertainty of a regime's intentions suggests that strict conditionality should prevail through the stabilization phase of economic reform. Given that stabilization mainly involves changing prices, there is no way to judge a government's long-term commitment to reform. However, once countries have embarked on true structural adjustment, changing economic institutions, the multilaterals should be looser with conditionality.

For Ghana, this perspective suggests that criticisms of IMF conditionality up to 1986 are probably overemphasized. There was no way for
the multilaterals to know how serious the Rawlings government was
about reform, and there were serious dangers to loosening conditionality
prematurely. Indeed, even the initial institutional reforms that the Ghanaians did make—eliminating price controls on some goods—could not
be viewed as a true gauge of their seriousness because these controls had
become largely irrelevant to the population at large. It was not until
1986 that Ghanaian officials introduced the first truly significant change
in economic institutions: the foreign exchange auction. Commitment to
the auction dramatically reduced uncertainty about the PNDC's determination to reform the economy and made it more difficult to backtrack
on those reforms. Until that point, however, strict conditionality was
justified.

Arguing that strict conditionality is justified until uncertainty is reduced does not mean that the IMF and World Bank cannot improve their
economic and public diplomacy—regardless of the good reasons, dealing not only with the individual country involved but also the multilaterals' entire lending program, for retaining strict conditionality. By
tying the degree of conditionality to the certainty of commitment to
reform, I am proposing an operationally realistic way that the multilateral organizations and African governments can foster reform. Unfortunately, those who simply suggest that the multilateral organizations
loosen their conditionality do not suggest how or by how much. Clearly,
ad hoc loosening of conditionalities not tied to a benchmark such as
institutional reform could be damaging to the multilateral organizations
as well as to proadjustment officials within individual African countries
who use conditionality requirements to promote reform within their
governments.

TIMING OF REFORMS

Orthodox economic reform programs attempt to address a significant
number of problems with a variety of instruments. Timing of those
instruments has naturally been a controversial issue. Killick, Bird, Sharp-
ley, and Sutton make the traditional case for a gradual implementation
of reforms:

> There must also be a general presumption in favor of gradual programs rather
> than shock treatment approaches [because of gestation lags]. . . . It also seems
> likely that the loss to "psychic welfare" is less when people have time to adjust

their lives to altered circumstances and policies than if traumatic changes are suddenly thrust upon them.[14]

Similarly, a U.S. congressional investigation of economic reform in Ghana and Senegal called for slower alleviation of external and internal deficits to minimize deflationary effects and pressures for rapid export growth.[15] Many governments in Africa have adopted this approach. For instance, to avoid unemployment and the resulting political pressures, Zimbabwe has implemented a program of gradual trade liberalization.[16]

In contrast, Lal argues that allowing people time to adjust may subvert the program:

The government may find that gradualism allows time for those hurt by the cuts to combine and exert irresistible pressure for their reversal. Politically, a long drawn out cut in real expenditures may thus be more difficult for a government to implement than a single, quick one.[17]

Between these two positions, there is a fundamental disagreement concerning whether it is politically desirable to implement a shock program and thereby prevent an opposing coalition from developing or to reform gradually and thereby forestall future protest by allowing people and firms time to adjust.

There is good reason to believe that stabilization measures should be "shock therapy." First, at least the initial economics of devaluation may require a shock program. Prolonged discussion and debate about devaluation measures in particular may cause speculation (because importers attempt to bring in more goods and exporters hold back goods) that significantly worsens the balance of payments problem.[18] As noted

14. Tony Killick et al., "The IMF: Case for a Change in Emphasis," in *Adjustment Crisis in the Third World,* ed. Richard E. Feinberg and Valeriana Kallab (New Brunswick: Transaction Books, 1984), 66. See also Frances Stewart, "Should Conditionality Change?" in *The IMF and the World Bank in Africa,* ed. Kjell J. Havnevik (Uppsala: Scandinavian Institute of African Studies, 1987), 41.

15. U.S. House Committee on Foreign Affairs, *Structural Adjustment in Africa: Insights from the Experience of Ghana and Senegal,* March 1989, 17.

16. "Zimbabwe Survey," *African Business,* June 1990, 21.

17. Lal, "Economic Liberalization," 275–76. Much the same position is adopted by Anne O. Krueger, "Interactions between Inflation and Trade Regime Objectives in Stabilization Programs," in *Economic Stabilization in Developing Countries,* ed. William R. Cline and Sidney Weintraub (Washington, D.C.: Brookings Institution, 1981), 112; and Martin Wolf, "Timing and Sequencing of Trade Liberalization in Developing Countries," *Asian Development Review* 4, no. 2 (1986): 13.

18. On speculative attacks and foreign exchange crises, see Sebastian Edwards, *The International Monetary Fund and the Developing Countries: A Critical Evaluation,* NBER Working Paper no. 2909 (Cambridge, Mass.: National Bureau of Economic Research, 1989), 16.

above, once a devaluation is implemented, a host of other policies have to be adopted at the same time if the change in the exchange rate is to have any effect.

Second, the shocks imposed by sudden stabilization programs may not be quite as great as the nominal magnitudes suggest because, as in the case of Ghana, a reforming government may, to some degree, simply be catching up with the shadow prices already being paid by most of the population. Also, as noted in chapters 3 and 4, there is substantial evidence indicating that analysts and African governments have overestimated the initial threat to political stability that may be caused by imposition of shock stabilization programs.

As governments move into the structural adjustment phase, the question of the timing of reform becomes more complicated. The Ghanaian experience indicates that it is important for a government to implement some reforms gradually so that it has time to survey the political situation and review its economic strategy. Also, reforms in the structural adjustment phase have to be more gradual because, as this examination of the Ghanaian case has stressed, changing long-standing economic institutions is an extremely difficult technical task that African governments are poorly equipped to do.

Even within the step-by-step process of exchange rate reform, however, as chapter 3 made clear, the Ghanaian government required a real strategy to deflect political pressure. A gradual adoption of reforms is no guarantee that opposition will not develop. Only if the government is able to intelligently use the time provided by a gradual approach will it be able to gain greater political acceptance. A strategy is especially important since even step-by-step reforms in the structural adjustment phase will inevitably produce shocks that the population will have difficulty absorbing. For instance, the Rawlings government instituted non-incremental devaluations at each new phase of the reform process.

The requirements for strategy are especially important because the Ghanaian experience suggests that in the long term it is difficult for governments to gain political support for structural adjustment. The logic of the gradualists depends on a government's being able to cultivate support for the reforms, which it could not do if there were shock reforms. However, as chapter 5 noted, it does not appear that this support will be gained easily, if for no other reason than that the institutional requirements needed to actually transmit support to the leadership are so great. Thus, gradual adoption of some reforms is not enough. A strategy must still be devised.

In addition, cultivating support for structural adjustment over time may be particularly difficult in Africa because, as a result of all the bottlenecks in the economies, it will not soon be evident who benefits from structural adjustment. In economies with relatively few distortions and in which factors of production (e.g., capital, labor) move relatively freely, it is immediately clear to most people who will benefit from drastic changes in government economic policy. However, because of the many distortions in African economies, even the winners (e.g., future owners of export industries) will not realize nearly as soon that they will benefit; therefore they may not initially support the government's reform program. Certainly in Ghana, even after the reform program had been in place for eight years, many entrepreneurs were not certain if they would benefit. A shock program would perhaps draw more adherents than a process of gradual reform because the former gives evidence sooner of who the winners are. Thus, the gradualist perspective may be less appropriate for African-type economies than it would be for, say, the more developed economies in Asia.

In their study of reform, Mosley, Harrigan, and Toye present a slightly different gradualist argument. They argue that losers and their representatives should be compensated by "non-distortive" payments.[19] They do not develop this idea, so it is unclear how they propose weak governments such as Ghana could adopt what appears to be an extremely complex program. Moreover, the analysis in this book suggests that such an approach would be unnecessary in Ghana and many other African countries. The potential losers in Ghana were not, after all, significant obstacles to reform. The analysis in previous chapters has suggested that because the economic decline had been so great and because so much of the real economy had already adjusted, there were far fewer who opposed the adjustment program than was originally thought. Indeed, compensating the losers might inadvertently provide a pole around which they could coalesce and oppose the adjustment program. Also, as indicated throughout this book, the administrative weaknesses of African countries are one of the chief obstacles to reform. Developing complex compensation schemes for losers who do not pose real political threats to the reform effort would therefore seem to be counterproductive.

The debate between those who would implement gradual reforms and those who advocate shock treatments therefore misses the point. In the

19. Ibid., 129.

beginning of an economic reform program, it is absolutely necessary, especially in the exchange rate area, to implement some shock reforms. However, during the long-term process of structural adjustment, administrative difficulties and the necessity to survey the population will force governments to choose a more gradual sequence of reforms. Obviously, this position corresponds closely with the argument made above on conditionality. Strict conditionality is most useful when shock treatments are needed; as a country proceeds through the reform program, the multilaterals' requirements can gradually be reduced. Indeed, during the initial stabilization phase, strict conditionality can be usefully implemented because numeric goals can be established for the money supply, exchange rate, and other prices the government sets. However, as will be argued below, once the difficult process of structural reform begins, reform goals cannot be quantified nearly as easily, so strict conditionality around unambiguous targets becomes less possible.

AFRICAN ECONOMIC REFORM AND THE INTERNATIONAL ECONOMY

Many critics of stabilization and structural adjustment cite the continuing influence of the international economy as a major constraint facing countries such as Ghana that are trying to reform. For instance, Jacques Pegatienan Hiey, in his study of Côte d'Ivoire, noted,

> The experience of the Ivory Coast illustrates a fundamental problem with IMF-type stabilization programmes. This is that the instruments recommended . . . have little impact on the principal constraints under which the economy functions, e.g., the level of import and export prices, the degree of dependence on foreign factors of production and interest rate structures in world financial markets.[20]

Hiey goes on to argue that the export emphasis of structural adjustment will cause African economies to become even more distorted.[21]

There are several immediate problems with this argument. First, it is little more than a truism that the international economy poses constraints on poor countries. Any reform program would face the same problems. If Ghana and other poor African countries are unusually vulnerable to the international economy, such vulnerability is in good part a result of government policies that kept them poor. Indeed, the

20. Jacques Pegatienan Hiey, *Ivory Coast* (Helsinki: WIDER, 1987), 36.
21. Ibid.

continual decline that African countries experienced may have made them more dependent on a few raw material exports. As exchange rates become overvalued, marginal exporting enterprises inevitably are less viable, leaving only the major raw material enterprises to increasingly dominate the declining export sector. For instance, in 1960, exports of all Ghanaian cocoa products (beans, paste, and butter) accounted for 59.7 percent of exports. Over the next two decades, there was a slow but significant increase in the share of cocoa products so that by 1978 cocoa comprised 69.9 percent of all exports.[22]

In contrast, structural adjustment programs have the potential to diversify African countries' export portfolio because devaluation may make exporting viable again. For instance, since the adoption of the ERP in Ghana, there has been a significant increase in mining investment, especially in gold, and some other export-oriented industries. Indeed, if cocoa prices do not increase from the levels they fell to in the late 1980s and gold prices are robust, there is a chance that gold could become Ghana's most important export by the mid-1990s. Given the economic role of cocoa in Ghana's history, such a diversification would have to be termed revolutionary. Decline, not structural adjustment, causes African countries to become ever more dependent on a few raw materials.

Perhaps even more important, critics such as Hiey ignore the fact that comprehensive economic reform of the type Ghana is attempting may also change government institutions and policies so that the dangers of being a raw material producer are mitigated. African countries face problems not because of their being monocrop or monomineral exporters per se but because of flawed government policies and the social conflicts that flow from dependence on relatively few goods. If Ghana and other African countries can change how they respond to the international economy, then the mere fact that they are raw material producers will become much less significant.

In fact, there are indications that Ghana is changing basic institutions and policies so that some of the disadvantages of being a primary commodity producer can be ameliorated. Ghana should be able to respond to international shocks—a continual danger to raw material exporters—much better than in the past because of the new policies it has adopted. In the late 1970s and early 1980s, African countries such as Ghana did not lower their exchange rate in response to exogenous

22. Kodwo Ewusi, *Statistical Tables on the Economy of Ghana, 1950–1985* (Accra: Institute of Statistical, Social and Economic Research, 1985), table 154.

shocks, thereby causing a real appreciation of the exchange rate and an eventual loss of market share in developed economies. Ghana was the extreme example of how disastrous this strategy was because its loss of share in the cocoa market propelled it into a downward spiral. In contrast, East Asian countries did markedly better by lowering their exchange rate and thereby gaining market share in the international economy.[23]

Another indication of the much healthier interaction between the Ghanaian economy and the international economy is the evolution of government finance. In the past, decreases in the price of cocoa inexorably led to government fiscal problems. Ghana's fiscal problems were severe in the early 1980s. However, in what could almost be called a revolutionary development given its chronic deficits in the early 1980s, in the late 1980s Ghana began to experience a surplus despite the decrease in the price of cocoa. The following list shows the government's deficits and surpluses as a percentage of total expenditures during that period.

1980	−38
1981	−59
1982	−50
1983	−33
1984	−18
1985	−16
1986	0
1987	4
1988	3[24]

In contrast, African countries' deficits averaged approximately 20 percent of total expenditures.[25] The surpluses run by the Ghanaian government suggest that the deepening of the tax base, in addition to fiscal controls and new emphasis on proper government policies, has had a dramatic effect on government finance. While Ghana will continue to be hurt by decreases in the prices of its exports, as any other country would be, it is unlikely that Ghana will experience the kind of chronic deficits

23. Moshin S. Khan, "Developing Country Exchange Rate Policy Responses to Exogenous Shocks," *American Economic Review* 76, no. 2 (May 1986): 86.

24. International Monetary Fund, *Government Finance Yearbook, 1990* (Washington, D.C.: IMF, 1990), 44, and ibid., *1991,* 32.

25. It should be noted that this average is calculated on the basis of a small number of countries. International Monetary Fund, *Government Finance Statistics Yearbook, 1990* (Washington, D.C.: IMF, 1990), 96.

caused in part by the kind of commodity price decreases that occurred before 1983. In addition, there is now at least some hope that the country will be able to handle commodity booms better.

DEPENDENCE ON AID

Finally, some have argued that the aid requirements of structural adjustment are so great that even reforming countries will remain dependent on the international economy. Also, a significant criticism of the Ghanaian experience has been that it has been driven mainly by World Bank and other donor aid at a level other countries could not expect to receive.

External aid has been an important part of the ERP since 1983, and foreign savings as a share of gross domestic product (GDP) are expected to rise from 4.4 percent in 1988 to 7.7 percent between 1989 and 1991 (see table 3).[26] There is no doubt that the World Bank's funding in particular has been critical to many specific projects and to lubricating the economic machinery at a time when many facets of the Ghanaian economy had all but stopped.

However, the aid Ghana has received is not that impressive when compared with that received by other African countries. Ghana's aid per capita doubled from approximately $13.3 per person in 1981 to $27.5 per person in 1987. It is this doubling to which so many attribute the success of the ERP. Still, $27.5 of aid per person is substantially below the $35.0 that African countries other than Nigeria averaged.[27]

Also, noting Ghana's dependence on aid is not a damning criticism of the ERP because the World Bank has made it clear from the beginning that economic reform in Africa would be dependent on a large inflow of resources from external donors at highly concessional rates.[28] Given the disrepair in which Ghana and other African countries have found themselves, there is no way they could have raised themselves by their own bootstraps. Aid can also be seen as a bridge to be used by African countries until governments can increase the amount of revenue they are able to raise from domestic sources.

A more serious question is whether or not the World Bank and other

26. Ghana, *Towards a New Dynamism: Report Prepared by the Government of Ghana for the Fifth Meeting of the Consultative Group for Ghana* (Accra: Ghana, 1989), 6.

27. All statistics in this and the following paragraph from World Bank, *African Economic and Financial Data* (Washington, D.C.: World Bank, 1989), 196–98.

28. World Bank, *Accelerated Development in Sub-Saharan Africa* (Washington, D.C.: World Bank, 1981), 121.

donors can provide the same level of resources to other African countries interested in following the Ghanaian model. Certainly (as noted in chapter 2), aid donors have committed a large amount of money to Africa over the last decade. There is probably more than enough money in the World Bank for five or six more Ghanas (as long as one of them is not Nigeria) because the money provided to Ghana, while large in African terms, was not that significant to the World Bank. Whether there will be funds for more countries than that is unclear. The lesson for African countries is that it is important to be the second or third fastest reformer rather than the twentieth. In a world where countries increasingly compete on the basis of economic reform, those African countries that act quickest will naturally be better off.

FUTURE RELATIONS WITH THE MULTILATERAL INSTITUTIONS

As noted throughout this book, the multilateral institutions have been central to the formulation, implementation, and financing of the ERP since it was adopted in 1983. Given the importance of multilateral funding, Ghana's relationship with the World Bank and the IMF may have been the single most salient aspect of its relationship with the world economy in the 1980s. Ghana's relationship with the multilaterals in the 1990s must be understood.

It is likely that Ghana will develop a much more normal relationship with the multilaterals in the 1990s. By "normal" I mean that, while the multilaterals will still be very important to Ghana, especially in financing, it is likely that they will become a less visible part of the policy process. The multilaterals will recede in prominence for several reasons. First, as noted above, Ghana is now well beyond the initial stabilization crisis where the IMF in particular has such an important role to play. In the early 1990s, the IMF apparently wanted Ghana to "graduate" back to the regular facilities used by most countries but was convinced that the country could still benefit from special terms. However, Ghana is clearly becoming more and more like most countries in the world in the IMF's view; consequently, the IMF's presence will certainly recede in the years to come.

Second, as the economy strengthens, the Ghanaians have also been able to significantly enhance their own economic decision-making structures. Thus, while the expertise provided by the World Bank and the IMF will be important, it will not be as crucial as it was in the early 1980s. For instance, during the first eight years of structural adjustment, the Bank of Ghana was able to enhance its administrative apparatus and is now taking on many of the true functions of a central bank, especially in supervising the banking system. Given how weak the central bank was before the ERP began, it could not have taken on this role before.

Third, as Ghana confronts the problems of structural adjustment, the IMF and the World Bank have fewer answers to the country's problems. The multilaterals could play an important role early in the stabilization crisis because of the power of their dogma. "Get prices right" is profound in its advice, persuasive to those who understand anything about the past distortions of the economy, and simple to convey. However, now that all of Ghana's prices are more or less correct (in the early 1990s, only the real interest rate, still negative, was noticeably off), the traditional type of advice that the IMF and the World Bank can offer will become much less important.

One example of the decreasing relevance of the multilaterals to Ghana's problems is the banking sector. The banking sector in Ghana presents a formidable obstacle to further growth. In particular, problems in the credit market have made it difficult for firms to raise capital to expand in response to the new productive economic environment the PNDC has established. At a more general level, the banking sector is interesting because it exemplifies the extremely difficult reforms that governments face once they go beyond stabilization and begin to try to reform fundamental economic structures.

The financial sector of the Ghanaian economy is extremely shallow. There is no capital market, and the stock exchange just began in late 1990. Banks must supply almost all the capital for companies wishing to expand. There are two private banks (Barclays and Standard Chartered) and six state-owned banks. Because of the dramatic changes in the economy since 1983, all the banks have a significant number of nonperforming loans. Businessmen who took out foreign-denominated loans when the cedi was 90 to the dollar, for instance, are facing a difficult repayment schedule with devaluation, especially if they are not exporters; by 1991, the cedi had reached 400 to the dollar. Further, the state-owned banks were until recently saddled with a large number of loans to SOEs that could not service their debts. Because the SOEs could not pay, the banks could not recycle loans, and there was a shortage of credit. This is an extremely common problem in many African countries. As Peter Nicholas noted, "The most difficult aspect of financial market and banking sector reforms has been ensuring an orderly transition for banking systems saddled with many nonperforming loans, sometimes of public enterprises, and liberalizing previously controlled lending and deposit rates."[29]

The problems of the banking sector are important to highlight because many in Ghana have argued that tight credit is a major barrier to expansion. For instance, the Ghana National Chamber of Commerce complained in a memo to the government,

> As we have stated often times recently, the greatest problem facing the Ghanaian businessman is low liquidity or the lack of it. . . . it has become increasingly difficult to obtain overdraft and credit facilities from the country's commercial banks as these banks have resorted to collecting previous loans more than granting new credit. . . . A lot of businesses are now faced with acute shortage of working capital and we are of the view that if the wheels of the economy are to be kept moving, businesses including industry and commerce should not be strangled to death.[30]

Similarly, John Richardson, president of the Association of Ghanaian Industries, has argued,

> Perhaps the most serious problem facing Ghanaian industry today is the problem of liquidity. It has been with us since the early days of the ERP. It has hardened in character over the past 6 years. . . . Our experience has been that as a result of several years of decline in productive activity, industrial establishments have been singularly ill-equipped to generate enough capital to meet their day to day operational requirements.[31]

Indeed, almost all businessmen will state that tight credit is the most formidable obstacle to their expansion or, in many cases, continued existence.[32]

It is important to note that the banks, especially the private ones, have a very different perspective on the credit problems of companies. Bankers fervently deny that there is any real credit problem for those who have going concerns. Rather, they argue that most of the Ghanaian

29. Peter Nicholas, *The World Bank's Lending for Adjustment*, World Bank Discussion Paper no. 34 (Washington, D.C.: World Bank, 1988), 20.
30. Ghana National Chamber of Commerce, "Memorandum on the Budget—1989," Accra, mimeo, 1989, 4.
31. John Richardson, "Speech at the 29th Annual General Meeting of the Association of Ghana Industries," Accra, mimeo, 1989, 8.
32. See also the study by William F. Steel and Leila M. Webster, *Small Enterprises in Ghana: Responses to Adjustment*, Industry and Energy Working Paper no. 33 (September 1990), 29.

private sector is essentially bankrupt and is made up of poor credit risks.[33] It is true that much of the private sector is corrupt and built upon the distortions of the 1960s and 1970s. Clearly, many of these companies will simply have to go out of business if the Ghanaian economy is to adjust to the new incentives the government has established.

The Ghanaian government has taken certain steps to begin reform of the banking sector. Most important, it has essentially written off the nonperforming debts of the SOEs by giving the banks government bonds in exchange for their paper. The government also hopes that the new stock market will grow rapidly from its narrow base in the years to come. Of course, in the early years the Ghanaian stock market will not be a very important institution but, as noted in chapter 6, over the next few decades, it could become absolutely crucial to the economy. The stock market will play a particularly important role in deepening the capital market because firms will no longer have to look only to the banks for capital.

However, far more remains to be done if the financial sector is to be liberalized so the economy can continue to grow. Private sector access to capital markets is a particularly important issue. Government officials such as Dr. Joseph Abbey speak of some type of "corporate PAM-SCAD," but they admit they are unsure of what to do.[34] Indeed, although everyone agrees that reform of the financial sector is probably the major problem facing the Ghanaian economy through the 1990s, there is great uncertainty about how the reforms should proceed.

The World Bank and the International Monetary Fund do not seem to have been particularly helpful to the government so far, and it is unclear if the multilaterals can provide more assistance in the future. The basic problem is that the multilaterals do not have a firm view of how African economies should operate once they are forced to go beyond "getting prices right." Therefore, in the area of financial sector reform, the multilaterals will play a much less prominent role. Indeed, their loss of prominence, especially compared to the role they played during the initial exchange rate, when IMF officials were critical in determining the magnitude of the first devaluation, is striking. The much lower profile of the multilaterals on banking reform will undoubtedly parallel experiences elsewhere in the economy as the Ghanaians confront issues of institutional change that require a great deal of local knowledge and analysis, exactly those areas in which the IMF and the World Bank are weakest.

33. Interviews, Accra, 15 August 1990.
34. Interview, London, 20 August 1990.

CONCLUSION

No reform program could quickly alter Ghana's or most other African countries' relationship with the world economy. The decline has been too great and the remaining institutions too weak to accomplish such a task. What is important is that the reform policies being adopted in Ghana and elsewhere will help African countries to cope much better with the constraints and opportunities posed by the international economy. The only real hope for African countries wishing to fundamentally change their relationship with the world economy is to reform and grow so that they will no longer have to continually plead for aid from the international community.

CHAPTER 8

Alternatives to Orthodox Economic Reform

The imposition of economic reform programs in Africa and the rest of the Third World has engendered a long debate since 1980. Many of the criticisms of adjustment—including claims that World Bank–inspired reforms impose significant hardships for large parts of the population—are true but do not offer guidance for policy analysis because they do not provide an alternative. Indeed, given the obvious weaknesses in African governments and markets, it is particularly easy to criticize any economic reform program suggested for Africa. Unfortunately, while criticizing the orthodoxy at length, many have offered no more than flimsy, unpersuasive suggestions to the policymaker trying to reform an economy such as Ghana's.[1]

Likewise, many of the proposed programs for economic reform assume that greater outside resources should be made available to Africa. This solution is equivalent to just wishing away a constraint that the multilaterals and African governments have to work with.[2] However, there have been a few more serious attempts at wholesale alternatives to orthodox economic reform. This book's in-depth analysis of the Ghanaian experience allows for an evaluation of the suggested alternatives.

1. For example, John Loxley and Bonnie K. Campbell argue that an alternative to structural adjustment would involve "guaranteeing minimum consumption levels." How this guarantee is supposed to be implemented is not revealed. See their "Introduction" in *Structural Adjustment in Africa*, ed. John Loxley and Bonnie K. Campbell (London: Macmillan, 1989), 9.

2. See the comments by Azizali F. Mohammed in *Africa and the International Monetary Fund*, ed. Gerald K. Helleiner (Washington, D.C.: IMF, 1986), 148.

AFRICA'S ECONOMIC ALTERNATIVE

African countries have repeatedly tried to develop their own collective alternative to proposals from the IMF and the World Bank. In 1980, the Organization of African Unity (OAU), in a document called *The Lagos Plan of Action,* laid down what it considered to be a strategy to promote economic growth for the next twenty years. As was the case with many documents from the Third World in the 1970s and early 1980s, the tendency of the Lagos Plan was to list the problems that African countries were facing, suggest a multitude of domestic reforms without even a vague hint of how these could be financed, and then recommend the creation of numerous international institutions to help African countries.

For example, in food agriculture, which the Lagos Plan isolates as crucial to future economic development, governments are supposed to improve the use of input packages; modify "techno-economic structures of production" to provide more incentives for farmers to increase production; use water better to irrigate lands; promote soil and water conservation; increase flood control and drainage; promote the use of improved hand tools; and develop physical infrastructure where necessary.[3] Why these measures should be taken and what priority should be given to them are never stated because the Lagos Plan does not suggest how the agrarian crisis the African states are facing originated.

The real emphasis of the Lagos Plan, however, is on restructuring the international institutions that govern African economic practices. The ultimate goal of the plan is to establish an African Common Market that would promote intracontinental trade by the year 2000. Along the way, numerous other institutions are suggested. In the area of trade and finance alone, the plan recommends creating an African Payments Union, an African Monetary Fund, and an African Guarantee Fund strengthening the African Development Bank.[4] While in good parts flights of fancy with no more than a few sentences to justify them, the Lagos Plan proposals do reflect the intellectual climate of the 1970s: the international economy was mainly to blame for Africa's economic crisis, and it was possible to modify this environment by creating a host of new institutions dominated by the South but, presumably, funded by the developed world. If it had not been for the World Bank, which published

3. Organization of African Unity, *Lagos Plan of Action* (Geneva: International Institute for Labour Studies, 1982), 10.
4. Ibid, xiii.

its highly controversial *Accelerated Development in Sub-Saharan Africa* at almost the same time, the Lagos Plan would have died a quiet, and unmourned, death.

Indeed, as African countries of all ideological stripes increasingly yielded to demands for reform in the mid-1980s, the debate over stabilization and structural adjustment programs became less strident. During the United Nations General Assembly's debate over Africa's economic crisis in 1986, the OAU put forth a document that, while still blaming the international economy for much of Africa's troubles, also acknowledged that many of the economic problems originated from the policies that African countries had adopted.[5] The OAU document explicitly embraced many of the reforms the World Bank had been promoting.

For instance, in the highly contentious area of exchange rate reform, the OAU noted that approximately twenty African countries had devalued, some several times. The OAU also restated African countries' commitment to demand management through budgetary reforms, reductions in the size of the civil service, and many other actions that the World Bank had suggested. While at the UN Africa made obsequious bows to the *Lagos Plan of Action,* it was clear that most countries on the continent were not putting much stock in the creation of a wide variety of international institutions and a continentwide common market to lift them out of their economic misery. At the same time, the OAU made it clear that reforms could not succeed unless the developed world markedly increased the amount of resources going to Africa through higher levels of aid and adoption of comprehensive programs of debt reduction. It was suggested at the UN that "Africa had done its part" and now it was time for the rest of the world to complete the bargain and increase aid.

Then, in July 1989, the UN Economic Commission for Africa (ECA) released its major document, *African Alternative Framework to Structural Adjustment Programmes for Socio-Economic Recovery and Transformation (AAF-SAP).* Although the ECA claimed that its new report was a continuation of the Lagos Plan and of Africa's 1986 submission to the UN, it had little to do with either of those documents. The *AAF-SAP,* while making a ritualistic bow to intracontinental cooperation, devotes most of its analysis to examining the domestic efforts that African

---

5. Organization of African Unity, *Africa's Submission to the Special Session of the United Nations General Assembly on Africa's Economic and Social Crisis* (Addis Ababa: OAU, 1986).

countries can undertake to resolve the economic crisis rather than hoping for the establishment of a large number of international institutions of the type that the Lagos Plan had envisioned. The new document also directly contradicts parts of Africa's 1986 submission to the United Nations, arguing that many of the orthodox reform programs the OAU had heralded African countries as accepting are flawed.

The title of the ECA paper suggests that the commission was aware of at least one of the problems with its previous analysis. By suggesting that it had an "alternative framework," the ECA was implicitly admitting the power of the neoclassical approach used by the World Bank and acknowledging that ad hoc attacks against the orthodoxy would not be persuasive. Only an entirely separate analysis, which suggested that African economies worked in ways fundamentally different from those described by the World Bank's analysis, would be persuasive.

The starting point of the ECA's document was that a neoclassical approach could not be applied to Africa. It criticized the World Bank and the IMF because

> the orthodox structural adjustment programmes, by their very design, assume that the classical instruments of control of money supply, credit squeeze, exchange rate and interest rate adjustments, trade liberalization etc. which may be valid in well-structured economies, could bring about positive results in African countries characterized by weak and disarticulate structures.[6]

The ECA was especially critical of reliance on foreign experts and managers in national economic decision making in Africa. Indeed, it seemed to blame the presence of foreigners more than such external factors as the debt burden for Africa's crisis.

The ECA document then critiqued the specific aspects of the World Bank–inspired programs. Inevitably, the document concentrated on exchange rate policies. The ECA first noted that because of "entrenched technological structures," devaluations will not have the intended effect of changing the orientation of African economies. It also noted that because many African nations are primarily producers of raw materials, devaluation will not foster exports because prices for these goods are determined outside the country. Finally, it claimed that devaluation caused inflation because imports become more expensive.[7]

---

6. Economic Commission for Africa, *African Alternative Framework to Structural Adjustment Programmes for Socio-Economic Recovery and Transformation (AAF-SAP)* (Addis Ababa: ECA, 1989), i.
    7. Ibid., 19.

In the same vein, the commission argued that the kind of "wholesale, indiscriminate, and doctrinaire privatization programs" recommended in many structural adjustment programs were harmful because African private sectors were not strong enough to take over public enterprises.[8]

The ECA's analysis is profoundly flawed. At the empirical level, some of its criticisms are simply not true. For instance, concerning structural adjustment policies, it is incorrect to say that the World Bank and the IMF have been forcing wholesale privatization policies on African countries. As noted in chapter 6, the World Bank has spent far more money helping African countries reform state-owned enterprises so they can operate more efficiently within the state than it has promoting privatization, although divestiture of state firms has received more press attention. This is certainly the case in Ghana, where the World Bank has had very limited expectations about privatization but has devoted a tremendous amount of money to reforming state-owned utilities and other parastatals. The alarmism of this charge is perhaps most of all a reflection of just how far the consensus over economic reform in Africa has broken down and of the ECA's determination to disagree with the World Bank and the IMF as much as possible, even if there is not really a clash.

More important, the ECA still suffers from the same problem it had when the *Lagos Plan of Action* was formulated: the commission does not, despite its title, provide a new framework of analysis for its proposals. Instead, what the *AAF-SAP* does is adopt the World Bank's framework of neoclassical microeconomics and then simply argue that there are exceptions to the model. This partial departure from the orthodoxy produces considerable confusion in the ECA's analysis, most notably in its view of the market. The rhetoric of the ECA document suggests that it believes that market forces work in a fundamentally different way in Africa. However, even a cursory examination of the commission's analysis indicates that the ECA is suggesting that the market does not work only when it is supposed to do something good; the commission is perfectly happy to believe that the market operates according to neoclassical models when a negative result is expected. For instance, while denying that the market forces operate according to orthodox models, the ECA says without hesitation that cuts in the fiscal deficit will be deflationary. Similarly, it is hard to understand how the commission can claim both that devaluations are inflationary and that they cannot have an effect on the relationship between prices and wages in African countries.

8. Ibid.

Much of the ECA's analysis is also often dangerously simplistic. For instance, it claims that because African countries have entrenched structures of production and are raw material producers (thus, price takers), devaluation will not positively affect the competitiveness of their goods. Even if this claim were 100 percent true (which it is not), it does not take account of a crucial argument for market-determined exchange rates: that even existing exporters will be hurt by an overvalued exchange rate and that a country will begin to lose its market share if its exporters cannot make a profit. For instance, Ghana, because of its long policy of overvalued exchange rates, lost a considerable share of the cocoa market even as it was becoming more dependent on that one crop. What the ECA does not seem to realize is that even if African countries have little to gain in the short run by ˙ ˙ ˙ ˙ting a market-determined exchange rate, they have much to lose if they continue to overvalue their currency.

The ECA's analysis that African economies are hampered by many bottlenecks in the end only suggests that the changes proposed by the World Bank and the IMF will take significantly longer than in developed countries where markets work more efficiently. The commission is saying, in effect, that the short term in Africa is much longer than in the developed world. If the World Bank in particular had stressed that change would come slowly in many African countries because of problems in the markets, this would not be a particularly profound criticism. However, the bank's eagerness to highlight the immediate impact of economic reform had the unexpected consequence of making the commission's criticisms appear much more damaging than they really are. This was especially true of the bank's 1989 publication, *Africa's Adjustment and Growth in the 1980's*, which tried to suggest, much earlier than was warranted, that World Bank programs were having a positive, noticeable effect on Africa countries.[9]

The question then becomes, Does the ECA have suggestions that would work better, faster? Some ECA recommendations do not clash with the thrust of World Bank programs. For instance, the ECA suggests a strong focus on agriculture including land reform and devoting increasing percentages of government budgets and foreign exchange to agriculture. The bank has also promised these reforms and is, just as the ECA suggests, planning to devote 20 percent of its Africa lending to agriculture.[10]

9. World Bank and UNDP, *Africa's Adjustment and Growth in the 1980's* (Washington, D.C.: World Bank, 1989).
10. See World Bank, *The Challenge of Hunger in Africa* (Washington, D.C.: World

Other aspects of the ECA's analysis are more problematic. On the exchange rate, for instance, the commission says that instead of devaluing, African countries should use multiple exchange rates "in a rationalized manner" and/or create "a system for purposes of resource transfers, resource mobilisation and reversal of capital flight and ensuring availability of essential imports."[11] What this means is exceptionally unclear; indeed, even the African ministers who reviewed the ECA document wanted the commission to reinforce this suggestion with further research and analysis. However, stressing the need for multiple exchange rates (with exporters presumably receiving less overvalued rates) implicitly contradicts the commission's previous analysis that African economies cannot respond to the incentives provided by devaluation.

The commission appears to be suggesting that governments allocate foreign exchange administratively using a variety of different rates and that they design those rates exactly according to the needs of the economy. Here the commission simply ignores the African experience over the last two decades—that government allocation of foreign exchange leads almost inevitably to damagingly overvalued rates because government officials are not under pressure to continually adjust their currencies in light of changes in inflation. Ghana is perhaps the paradigmatic example of the problems that administratively determined exchange rates can cause. Also, when governments post exchange rates, especially in the kind of complex multiple-tier system the ECA suggests, the administrative apparatus that needs to be established almost always becomes a significant constraint on business because African governments do not have the manpower or the administrative structures to handle the large number of foreign exchange applications in anything approaching an efficient manner. Applications for crucial imports languish for months as bureaucracies are unable to micromanage large parts of the economy by deciding which uses of foreign exchange are valid and what rate of local currency potential importers should pay. Finally, there are immense incentives for corruption in multiple-tier systems because the government is allocating a scarce resource. Many businesses cannot afford the delay and capriciousness that the administrative allocation of foreign exchange introduces and are willing to pay extra for what they need or want.

Bank, 1988), 5; and Ismail Serageldin, *Poverty, Adjustment and Growth in Africa* (Washington, D.C.: World Bank, 1989), 14–15.

11. ECA, *Alternative Framework,* 40.

The ECA noted early in its document that African economic institutions are already severely overburdened. Yet the ECA, which was realistic about the performance of African markets, seems not at all concerned about the performance of African states even though over the last two decades all evidence suggests that this performance has been abysmal. Indeed, in countries such as Ghana, the administrative apparatus had all but broken down and, even after almost a decade of structural adjustment, is still exceptionally weak. As chapter 6 notes, what critics of flawed markets forget is that they are really choosing between imperfect markets and imperfect governments.

ADJUSTMENT WITH A HUMAN FACE

During the late 1980s, orthodox economic reform also came under criticism from many other analysts. The first, and perhaps most important, salvo was fired by officials based at UNICEF who claimed that implementation of structural adjustment policies placed an unusually heavy burden on the poor and disadvantaged in developing countries. In their major document, *Adjustment with a Human Face,* Giovanni Andrea Cornia, Richard Jolley, and Frances Stewart argued that the costs placed on the poor in structural adjustment programs were just too great because decreases in government subsidies, drastic cuts in social programs, and implementation of disinflationary macroeconomic programs posed life-threatening dangers to women, children, and the aged. They reasoned that it was time to move away from conventional approaches to adjustment and toward an adjustment process that focused clearly on the needs of the poorest groups.[12]

The tone of the document, and much of the "human face" analysis that followed, was that of a clarion call for a radically different approach to the economic needs of poor countries. However, if the tone and some of the more outlandish rhetoric is put aside, it is clear that, at most, the authors of *Adjustment with a Human Face* were arguing for a modification of the World Bank/IMF approach while retaining the most important macroeconomic reforms of orthodox economic reform policies. That the UNICEF approach was simply a call for modification, rather than overthrow, of the economic orthodoxy became inevitable as soon as the authors recognized that they would have to focus on adjustment,

12. Giovanni Andrea Cornia, Richard Jolley, and Frances Stewart eds., *Adjustment with a Human Face,* vol. 1(Oxford: Clarendon Press, 1987), 131–35.

rather than development or some other goal, and that they would have to situate their analysis within the framework of neoclassical economics. Indeed, they argued with a realism that has escaped many who simply follow their rhetoric that the economic crisis of the 1970s and early 1980s, not the policies of the multilateral organizations, caused most of the suffering of the vulnerable groups:

> We recognize that the primary cause of the downward economic pressure on the human situation in most of the countries affected is the overall economic situation, globally and nationally, not adjustment policy as such. Indeed, without some form of adjustment, the situation would often be far worse.[13]

Unfortunately, others have simply latched onto the "human face" bandwagon without realizing that it is, at most, a modification of the traditional reform programs advocated by the World Bank and the IMF.[14]

Many of the other UNICEF recommendations do not contradict the bank's overall macroeconomic approach if for no other reason than that they are unclear or so couched in reservations that (unlike the rhetoric) they could not clash with any proposed economic policy. For instance, the UNICEF authors recognize that the higher agricultural producer prices that are an integral part of most economic reform policies are beneficial to vulnerable groups dependent on farming. At the same time, higher food prices will hurt poor groups in the urban areas, which have to buy food. Faced with this contradiction, the UNICEF study simply advises policymakers to use "careful analysis."[15]

The UNICEF study makes its greatest contribution to the debate on economic reform by calling for the establishment of special programs to help the poor. The reforms advocated include increasing the amount of money spent on health and education going to the poorest and reforming these interventions so that they are cost-efficient and reach the largest number of people possible.[16] These proposals are a clear *addition* to World Bank proposals for structural adjustment, which up to the late 1980s did not include these kinds of compensatory programs. In part, the bank's failure to initiate the kinds of reforms UNICEF suggested was a result of the bank's not focusing on the welfare of vulnerable groups. Also, the bank seriously underestimated how long adjustment was going to take and therefore downplayed the short-term negative effects on

---

13. Ibid., 5.
14. See, for instance, the Khartoum Declaration, ambitiously titled "Towards a Human-Faced Approach to Socio-Economic Recovery and Development in Africa," U.N. General Assembly Document A/43/430, annex I, 29 June 1988.
15. Ibid., 160.
16. Ibid., 159.

women, children, and the aged. Finally, the administrative requirements of programs to help the poor are necessarily large, and countries such as Ghana simply did not have the bureaucratic wherewithal to implement these types of policies while trying to adopt the other extremely difficult aspects of a structural adjustment program.

However, an approach that focuses simply on poverty is misdirected given the magnitude of Africa's economic problems. Indeed, some critics of structural adjustment seem to ignore the monumental problems that African economies face when they concentrate solely on poverty. The reality is that African countries are at the economic precipice. If they do not begin to grow immediately, they face not only the prospect of declining living standards but also the possibility of national disintegration. Countries that are already poor simply cannot afford further decline. The chaos in countries such as Sudan, Liberia, and Somalia may very well be the future for the rest of the continent unless growth resumes. The Ghanaian experience up to 1983 clearly suggests that as national economic and administrative systems disintegrate there is no chance of helping the poor. Inevitably, therefore, addressing distributive questions is less important than implementing policies that help to preserve the economic and administrative integrity of the nation.

Also, the discussion of adjustment hurting the "poorest"—Toye, for instance, notes that one of the problems of Ghana's Economic Recovery Programme in the early years was that the poor lost out relatively[17]— fundamentally confuses issues of poverty in Africa. As Dr. Abbey noted,

> People who live in rich countries see poverty as pathological which can be solved through policies. Those who object to people living in cardboard houses in rich countries come to Africa and think that they are seeing the same thing when they see people living in cardboard. A focus on the poor tends to put problems of redistribution at center of political debate rather than question of production.[18]

In fact, almost everyone in Ghana, and almost all other African countries, is poor on any objective basis. Therefore, the fact that adjustment programs may not always directly benefit the absolutely poorest should have far less policy and moral implications than if there were a bias in a rich country. If adjustment programs help a significant number of people in Africa, then inevitably a large number of the poor will be helped.

In particular, economic growth in the rural sector—where most of the

---

17. John Toye, "Ghana," in *Aid and Power*, vol. 2, ed. Paul Mosley, Jane Harrigan, and John Toye (New York: Routledge, 1991), 169.
18. Interview, London, 20 August 1990.

poor in Africa live—is absolutely crucial to any kind of program to alleviate poverty.[19] Thus, one study found that in Ghana 80 percent of the poor and almost all of the poorest are in the rural areas outside Accra.[20] In the vast majority of African countries, better prices for farmers and improved agrarian services—the very heart of most orthodox economic programs—do more to alleviate poverty than do government-provided social services.

Actual growth in the rural sector is especially important because government-sponsored programs to alleviate poverty seldom, if ever, affect the truly poor, especially in Africa, where governments' administrative infrastructure outside the major cities ranges from weak to altogether absent. For instance, a study of the poor in Côte d'Ivoire found that the establishment of user fees for medical care would not affect the truly poor because they seldom had access to a doctor or a nurse for their ailments.[21] Similarly, decreases in public sector employment will not affect the truly poor because they are seldom, if ever, employed by government. The Côte d'Ivoire study found that if *all* the heads of poor households who worked for government were to lose their jobs, only 2 percent of the poorest 30 percent of the population and only 1 percent of the poorest 10 percent would be affected.[22]

Similarly, PAMSCAD—Ghana's major effort to help the poor—has been bedeviled by administrative problems since it was first proposed in 1988. Indeed, a program such as PAMSCAD, which requires literally hundreds of administrative systems in the rural areas, is precisely the kind of program that a government in a country such as Ghana finds most difficult to implement. It is for this reason that PAMSCAD will, to a great extent, always be an add-on to an economic reform program.[23] In

19. This point is missed by those who simplistically claim that adjustment programs will automatically hurt the poor. See, for instance, Robert Fatton, Jr., "Liberal Democracy in Africa," *Political Science Quarterly* 105, no. 3 (Fall 1990): 469.

20. E. Oti Boateng et al., *A Poverty Profile for Ghana, 1987–1988,* Social Dimensions of Adjustment in Sub-Saharan Africa, Working Paper no. 5 (Washington, D.C.: World Bank, 1990), 14. Similarly, in a survey of Côte d'Ivoire, researchers found that while 59 percent of all Ivorians live in the rural areas, 86 percent of the poorest 30 percent of the population and 96 percent of the poorest 10 percent of the population live outside the cities. Paul Glewwe and Dennis de Tray, *The Poor during Adjustment: A Case Study of Côte d'Ivoire,* Living Standards Measurement Survey Paper no. 47 (Washington, D.C.: World Bank, 1988), 13.

21. Ibid., 28.

22. Ibid., 15.

23. Richard Jolley criticizes PAMSCAD for being an addition to the ERP but ignores the tremendous administrative constraints that Ghana is operating under. Richard Jolley, "Poverty and Adjustment in the 1990's," in *Strengthening the Poor: What Have We*

addition, almost inevitably, administrative requirements and political pressure divert money for programs to help the poor to political purposes. For instance, much of the PAMSCAD money has actually been used to help alleviate the government's political problems by providing disgruntled Ghanaians with side payments. Even some government officials have questioned why civil servants who have been fired should have the benefit of PAMSCAD programs when the far more numerous Ghanaians who never enjoyed the largesse of a state position in the first place do not have access to PAMSCAD programs.[24]

More generally, PAMSCAD resources are directed to areas where the state already has a relatively strong administrative apparatus—that is, the areas that have traditionally benefited from government programs. Thus, PAMSCAD, which was supposed to direct all its resources to the impoverished north, has now been expanded to the entire country, and the resources are spread very thin indeed. In contrast, putting money directly into the hands of the rural poor by making the economic activities they engage in more rewarding would do far more for them than whatever government programs can be adopted by African states, which are usually highly unorganized at the rural level.

It is also important to note that ad hoc programs to alleviate poverty sponsored by aid donors and governments are no substitute for long-term economic growth, which allows for the natural establishment of social services in a more lasting manner. For instance, the conventional wisdom is that Kenya has adopted a long-term policy of economic growth at the expense of social services while Tanzania, though sacrificing some prosperity, has been more successful in devoting resources to social welfare programs. However, an examination of the actual statistics suggests that because Kenya's overall economic policies promoted economic growth and a relatively prosperous government financial base over a long period, it not only has a much higher gross national product per capita than Tanzania (US$ 360 versus US$ 130 in 1989), but it also has developed a better social service base. Life expectancy at birth is 59 years in Kenya compared to 49 years in Tanzania, while in Kenya, in 1988, 93 percent of all children were in primary schools compared to approximately 66 percent in Tanzania. Only about 4 percent of all

Learned? ed. John Lewis (Washington, D.C.: Overseas Development Council, 1988), 171. Other UNICEF documents call PAMSCAD "a good example of what is meant, in practice, by 'adjustment with a human face.'" UNICEF, *The State of the World's Children 1990* (New York: UNICEF, 1990), 10.

24. Interview, Ministry of Finance, Accra, 25 July 1989.

eligible children in Tanzania attend secondary school as opposed to 23 percent in Kenya.[25]

Finally, the elimination of distortions in an economy can also have a beneficial impact on the poor. For instance, because almost all basic goods had to be purchased on the black market in Ghana by the early 1980s, the poor were probably paying above the market clearing price. The black-market price includes a risk premium and a rent component derived by those with privileged access to goods. Liberalization of price controls may therefore have actually eased poor people's access to goods, a fact obscured by official inflation figures, which primarily examine controlled prices.[26] Similarly, strengthening the collection of revenue by the Ghanaian government through such measures as devaluation may have an impact on the poor because the government will, in the long term, be able to spend more on social services.

One of the greatest dangers in analyzing Africa is applying Western preconceptions to the process of development. While distributional issues should be a particular concern in the developed world, transferring this attitude to Africa without recognizing the fundamentally different context is a mistake. Given the enormous deprivations in Africa, there is no way that the poor will be helped in a meaningful way unless the national economy of Ghana and other African countries is improved.

CONCLUSION

The intellectual dominance of the World Bank and the IMF should be worrisome even to those who believe that many of their current recommendations are correct. The history of development over the past thirty years is, in good part, a succession of dominant ideas (e.g., import-substitution, basic human needs) being overturned. In the early 1990s, structural adjustment has at least the intellectual dominance of previous conventional wisdoms. This stature comes about not only because of the strength of the classical foundations of structural adjustment but also because the major alternatives, including those analyzed in this chapter, do not persuasively address the challenges that African countries face. It is to be hoped that Africans and others concerned with the political

25. World Bank, *World Development Report 1991* (Washington, D.C.: World Bank, 1991), 204, 260.
26. Peter S. Heller et al., *The Implications of Fund-Supported Adjustment Programs for Poverty: Experiences in Selected Countries,* International Monetary Fund Occasional Paper no. 58 (Washington, D.C.: IMF, 1988), 17.

economy of development will soon formulate ideas that can construc-
tively challenge the current intellectual dominance of the World Bank
and the IMF. However, any new set of proposals must be based on a
realistic evaluation of the capacities of states and markets in Africa and
must recognize Africa's desperate economic situation.

CHAPTER 9

The Challenges of Economic Reform and the Future of the African State

The previous eight chapters have provided a comprehensive review of the Ghanaian experience since the inception of the Economic Recovery Programme. On this foundation, it is now possible to make some generalizations about the political challenges of reform in Ghana and also in other Third World countries that are confronting many of the same problems the PNDC has encountered. While no two countries' political situations are exactly alike, the economic problems that confront Ghana, as stressed throughout this book, are similar to those of other African countries, and the array of policy responses the World Bank and the IMF have recommended are certainly applicable to other countries.

THE POLITICAL CHALLENGE OF REFORM

Much of the literature on economic reform suggests that leaders face great societal pressures when trying to adopt a reform program. Many studies therefore search for factors—such as political strength of the leader or the cohesion of the senior economic team—that would mitigate this societal pressure. In Ghana, however, alienating important constituencies turned out to be much less important than usually thought because when the state reaches a certain stage of decline, interest group pressures on the state may be significantly weaker than is traditionally pictured.

While scholars have noted the importance of patron-client relationships in the "soft" African state, they have also noted that strategies of withdrawal, as people try to escape from the predatory grasp of the state, are common. In Ghana, these withdrawal strategies took the form of paying black-market prices for desperately needed goods, working in the informal sector, and adopting a whole range of what Chazan calls "suffer-manage" techniques.[1] Clearly, to the extent that citizens withdraw from the state, they lessen their dependence on patron-client ties; they therefore may not have much stake in pressuring the state to change its economic policies. Indeed, in Ghana by the early 1980s, the economy had deteriorated to such an extent that even senior government officials, who normally benefit from access to imported goods even in times of shortage, reported that they were going hungry and were concerned that they could not find food for their families. As the state disintegrates and patron-client relationships dependent on state largess become relatively less rewarding compared to withdrawal, paradoxically the potential for the leadership to enact significant economic reforms may become greater.

The importance of withdrawal to subsequent reform efforts is also particularly significant given the assumptions of the new institutional economics. Borrowing from developed countries' experiences, Eggertsson notes that "all rulers depend on the support of influential social groups to maintain their power."[2] In Ghana, this simply was not true. The Rawlings regime was placed in power through the efforts of part of the military and managed to stay in power, in good part, because no influential social group had the willingness and/or the ability to try to affect who was in power.

As a result, while new instabilities may eventually appear, it is probably easier than originally thought for many governments to enact initial stabilization programs, especially if they are politically astute. As this book has stressed, the nominal magnitudes of price changes during stabilization programs are often somewhat misleading because much of the real economy has adjusted to shadow prices. In addition, the international community has demonstrated that it is willing to devote substantial resources to those African countries that demonstrate serious efforts to reform their economies. Thus, the early preoccupation with "IMF riots" did not focus on the real important political aspects of economic reform in African countries.

1. Naomi Chazan, *An Anatomy of Ghanaian Politics: Managing Political Recession, 1969–1982* (Boulder: Westview, 1982), 316.
2. Thrainn Eggertsson, *Economic Behavior and Institutions* (Cambridge: Cambridge University Press, 1990), 328.

THE ECONOMIC CONSEQUENCES OF REFORM

That a government is able to enact initial reform measures does not necessarily mean it has met the most difficult challenges posed by reform. Indeed, it is the long effort to adjust fundamental institutions that will cause the most significant problems for African countries. It is particularly important to understand just what economic reform has meant to the Ghanaian economy, and will mean to other countries attempting to adjust, because the magnitude of the benefits will naturally affect the politics of reform. Examining the economic benefits of reform is also critical because the polemics of both proponents and opponents of reform in Africa tend to obscure a more complex reality.

At the most general level, the Ghanaian economy between 1983 and 1991 grew at an average rate of approximately 5–6 percent. This is a spectacular performance considering that the rest of the continent (excluding Nigeria) grew by only 2.3 percent a year between 1980 and 1987.[3] However, these growth statistics should be considered in context. Figure 6 indicates that, while there has been an increase in the real per capita income of Ghanaians, the 1991 income level increase only returned the country to where it had been in 1982. The average Ghanaian's income was approximately 125 percent higher in 1971 than in 1991. Other indicators of economic activity also suggest that the Ghanaian economy is only slowly recovering. For instance, total electrical generation in 1988 was only 91 percent of what it had been in 1980.[4] Indeed, it will take many years of high economic growth just for the economy to return to 1957 levels.

There is a good argument to be made that, for the Ghanaian economy, 5–6 percent annual growth simply is not good enough. Three percentage points of that growth is taken up by population growth. Approximately one and one-half percentage points should be saved if the economy is going to fund enough investment to grow in the future. This means that personal consumption probably can increase by only one and one-half percentage points each year. At this rate, it will take a decade or more for Ghana to get back to the consumption levels of the early 1970s, which were hardly impressive. City-dwellers, who have been relatively hurt by the change in the rural-urban terms of trade, probably have not, on

3. The continent including Nigeria grew by only .5 percent each year. World Bank, *Sub-Saharan Africa: From Crisis to Sustainable Growth* (Washington, D.C.: World Bank, 1989), 222.

4. Statistical Services, *Quarterly Digest of Statistics* 6, no. 4 (Accra: Statistical Services, 1988), 14.

average, seen a significant rise in their personal consumption levels. Thus, while Ghana is viewed as a success by aid donors, the people at the lower economic levels will only slowly begin to receive the benefits of the reforms.

To its credit, the PNDC has acknowledged that consumption levels are low and has tried to reduce expectations concerning future gains. For instance, Flt. Lt. Rawlings has repeatedly stated that he understands that many Ghanaians are still suffering, despite the international acclaim for the ERP. In his 1990 New Year speech he said,

> Notwithstanding the vast improvement in the supply of goods and services in the markets today, there are many who have found it difficult during the past holiday season to manage a modest celebration with a chicken for a meal.[5]

Dr. Joseph Abbey suggested that the PNDC is aware of the low consumption levels and believes that 10 percent growth would be necessary if personal consumption levels were to increase at a rate the PNDC viewed as acceptable.[6] Thus, while Ghana has achieved considerable success at 6 percent a year, even this performance should be seen as inadequate to some degree. Also, it should be clear that Ghana and other African countries will have to continue with structural adjustment programs for many years before their citizens see significant benefits.

The inability of the Ghanaian economy to do more faster is taken by some critics to mean that the ERP has not been a success. However, it is difficult to imagine how the Ghanaian economy could have done any better over the last few years. Ghana did not have the physical or human infrastructure to achieve the admirable levels of growth of the newly industrializing countries in Asia. Indeed, given the decay that the government and private sector experienced in Ghana during the 1970s and early 1980s, 6 percent may have been the maximum possible growth, at least in the early years of the recovery program. Even in the early 1990s, the Ghanaian government was having great problems with basic administrative issues posed by the growing economy.

Therefore, there should be greater realism when estimating what structural adjustment can and cannot accomplish. Clearly, the major goal for African reform during the 1990s will be to get economies back to where they were in the early or mid-1960s. While rehabilitation and reversing past declines will only begin to address the enormous economic problems that African countries face, the economic and administrative

5. *People's Daily Graphic,* 4 January 1990.
6. Interview, London, 20 August 1990.

infrastructures of these countries must be restored before growth can begin again. That more cannot be done faster is perhaps the most tragic result of Africa's long decline.

The fact that the benefits of economic reform will take an exceptionally long time to become apparent has important political ramifications. It has long been recognized that stabilization and structural adjustment programs impose large costs in the short term. For instance, devaluation increases costs for importers immediately. However, it was felt that the reforms would become more palatable as the economic benefits became more apparent. Thus, political support for reform would grow as net exporters expanded production and employed more people.

This book suggests that it will take even longer than originally expected for those benefits to become visible and, correspondingly, for a solid constituency in favor of structural adjustment to coalesce. In addition, as noted in chapter 5, the absence of institutional ties with the groups that benefit from reform will also impede the development of politically meaningful support for economic reform. Finally, African countries will always be vulnerable to exogenous shocks from the international economy (e.g., the sudden drop in the price of cocoa) that will cause their economies to deteriorate. That structural adjustment will allow African countries to weather these shocks better than they did before may be of little comfort to citizens concerned more with their deteriorating standard of living than with the fact that their countries are doing better than they would have done under an alternative set of policies. As a result, there may be, as there is in Ghana, only grudging acceptance of the reform program.

THE STRUCTURAL ADJUSTMENT OF POLITICS

Focusing on the limited long-term gains yielded by structural adjustment sets the context for understanding the major political challenge of reform: to fundamentally alter the way the state operates later in reform programs so that true structural adjustment can evolve. As was noted in chapters 3 and 4, the kind of closed, authoritarian governments willing to use political repression, such as the PNDC, are in some ways well suited to implementing controversial stabilization measures. However, precisely because it is closed and authoritarian, it will be extremely difficult for the PNDC, or other such African governments, to enact the reforms required in the structural adjustment phase unless the state becomes more decentralized, develops better ties with civil society, and is able to gather and process more information.

For instance, the efforts to promote reform and privatization of the SOEs have encountered significant problems because of the PNDC's unwillingness to devolve political authority and decision making. Because an effective barrier has not been established between government ministries and the SOEs, politicians can impose noncommercial demands on the companies. Indeed, there are reports that the parastatals are having trouble attracting qualified managers because skilled Ghanaians do not want to enter companies where politics plays such an important part.[7]

Similarly, the government's efforts to privatize have been blocked by its centralized nature. The Divestiture Implementation Committee (DIC), formerly part of the State Enterprise Commission, was seen as largely ineffectual. The DIC was therefore removed from the Enterprise Commission and placed under the leadership of senior PNDC officials with the idea that the DIC could make the majority of decisions on privatization without having to consult the PNDC itself. In practice, however, all issues of privatization are still referred to the PNDC, where applications often languish. It appears that the leadership still views privatization as too sensitive an issue to leave to lower-ranking officials.[8] This problem is, as noted in chapter 6, aggravated by the fact that the PNDC has not developed a vision of the economic frontiers of the state that would allow lower-ranking officials to proceed on the privatization issue.

The banking sector also demonstrates the difficulties African governments face once they progress beyond the stabilization phase. Reforms such as the liberalization of the banking sector involve very difficult problems; solving them requires vast amounts of information, analysis, and administrative talent, all of which are lacking in Ghana and in other African countries. If these abilities are going to be developed, the government must decentralize its decision-making authority and develop much denser ties to civil society. Otherwise, complex reforms of the banking sector, or other aspects of the economy, cannot proceed because top policy officials will not have the time or knowledge to micromanage every aspect of the reform. If the leadership should become involved in

7. Interviews, Accra, 13 and 14 August 1990.
8. Interviews, Accra, 13 and 14 August 1990.

the minutiæ of the complex policy changes, they will not have sufficient time to address other important national issues.

The problem of style of government is particularly important because African governments do not face the question of simply "sustaining" reforms as an adjustment program continues. Rather, reform programs constantly face new challenges which must be overcome if growth is going to continue and to accelerate. Of course, the discovery of new challenges is only natural as a country moves from stabilization to structural adjustment because the correction of distorted prices allows policymakers to understand, perhaps for the first time, the fundamental problems of their economic institutions. Further, as some economic institutions are reformed, it becomes apparent that, even in a simple economy such as Ghana's, other economic institutions will also have to be transformed if growth is going to proceed.

If the new challenges are not met through innovative government responses then the country will, at best, continue with a moderate growth rate that will not markedly affect personal consumption in the short to medium term. At worst, failure to meet the new challenges encountered during structural adjustment could cause the reform program to grind to a halt. Thus, a country desperate for economic reform must have the appropriate type of government at every stage of the reform process or face the possibility of renewed stagnation and decline.

"AUTHORITARIAN" VS. "DEMOCRATIC" GOVERNMENTS DURING REFORM

Understanding the contrast in the political styles necessary for stabilization and structural adjustment should help answer the seemingly endless debate on whether authoritarian or democratic governments are better at adopting adjustment programs.[9] In fact, the debate to some extent is pointless because the political requirements of reform vary so dramatically over time. Accordingly, different types of governments will be better or worse at distinct types of reform. As in so many cases, attempts at grand generalizations not only are wrong but also miss a more subtle point crucial to understanding the political dynamics at work.

While this book has stressed the advantages authoritarian govern-

9. One particularly good review of the question is Stephan Haggard and Robert Kaufman, "The Politics of Stabilization and Structural Adjustment," in *Developing Country Debt and Economic Performance*, vol. 1, ed. Jeffrey D. Sachs (Chicago: University of Chicago Press, 1989), 233.

ments have during stabilization, there is not enough evidence from Africa to suggest that democracies cannot introduce significant price reforms. Ideally, however, if a country does have an authoritarian government during the stabilization period, that government would give way immediately to a decentralized democratic one with enough links to civil society to handle the complex structural adjustment program. Of course, no country can actually plan such a transition. Rather, the question is whether authoritarian governments such as the PNDC can transform themselves to meet the new political challenges of sustained reform.

In the case of the PNDC, even absent the democratic pressures that emerged in the early 1990s, it is doubtful if the transition to a regime more appropriate for structural adjustment could have been made. Rawlings often ignored the contradictions between his authoritarian practices and the political requirements of structural adjustment, apparently believing he could manage the conflict between rhetoric and reality by exerting his personal "charisma." The leader of the PNDC is constantly pictured interacting with the population, and there is no doubt that he has his pulse on popular opinion. Despite Rawlings's apparent popularity, however, there is little evidence that his personal following is strong enough to overcome the very real political challenges the PNDC faces. The political problems of transformation Rawlings faces center on the necessity of making fundamental changes in institutions so that the state can operate in a different manner. Personal followings may ease transitions but are not a substitute for these institutional changes.

The authoritarian PNDC also is unable to develop a political vocabulary to justify its new program. Economic reform as championed by the World Bank has yet to develop a political vocabulary. Indeed, as noted in chapter 4, the PNDC has even attempted to gain legitimacy by resurrecting Nkrumah—although its economic policies are the exact opposite of what Ghana's first leader offered the country.

Finally, the political challenges of stabilization in particular may have had far more appeal to Rawlings personally than the more difficult reforms that have to be brought about for structural adjustment. Rawlings came into politics as an angry young man intent on doing something to reverse his country's long-term decline. That the program he eventually latched onto was economically conservative may have been less important than that it offered him the chance to bring about radical reforms in the authoritarian style he was used to. Indeed, the reforms the PNDC brought about have been, as stressed repeatedly in this book,

revolutionary even if they are not leftist. However, the political challenges that structural adjustment demand do not promise the kind of
quick, gratifying changes that the stabilization measures offered. The
measures needed for structural adjustment are difficult to implement and
do not lend themselves to Rawlings's authoritarian style. Indeed, given
that structural adjustment demands some kind of political opening, the
reforms will inevitably bring back certain practices, and perhaps person-
alities, that Rawlings and the rest of the PNDC associate with the
excesses and failures of civilian rule. Thus, the angry young military man
is far better at stabilization than at structural adjustment.

More generally, the Ghanaian case suggests that it will be very difficult for any authoritarian government to reform itself sufficiently to be
well suited to implement the difficult policies of structural adjustment.
First, as noted throughout this study, the authoritarian actions taken
while reforming prices will often come back to haunt governments later
when they are attempting to develop a dense network of ties with civil
society in order to implement reforms requiring large amounts of information. Second, as with the PNDC, authoritarian governments simply
may not be able to change their political style and vocabulary in order to
reform basic institutions. Indeed, the characteristics of authoritarian
regimes that successfully change prices—obstinacy, determination to
implement a single goal—seem to militate against an easy transformation into a flexible regime able to reform institutions.

DEMOCRACIES AND ECONOMIC REFORM

However, it should not be assumed that a democratically elected government in Ghana will automatically be able to proceed with structural
adjustment. In particular, the assumption that, as William Foltz has
noted, "all good things go together" more or less automatically needs to
be challenged. Ghana presents a good case on which to base some
concrete propositions about the relationship between political and economic change. Perhaps the most important contribution the Ghana case
can make is to move the discussion of democratization beyond the label
of "multiparty elections." To some, multiparty elections are synonymous
with democracy; to others, they are an essential ingredient. The stress on
multiparty elections as the only true indicator of democracy has become
stronger as a result of the 1989 revolutions in Eastern Europe. As a
result, many inside and outside Africa are suddenly demanding that

African countries institute political systems based on electoral competition.

However, as Ghana and many other African countries' histories demonstrate, simply having the form of multiparty democracy does not guarantee either a well-functioning polity or economic progress. Multiparty systems failed throughout Africa in the early 1960s, and there is very little reason to believe they will succeed in the 1990s if just their form is adopted. Many other aspects of a democratic polity are important, although they do not carry the glamor of multiparty elections. Unfortunately, many seem to believe that these other aspects of a democratic polity will be automatically instituted if the form of multiparty elections is adopted. The poor record of multiparty systems in Ghana, Nigeria, and other countries in Africa suggests otherwise. Indeed, given that the history of multiparty elections is so limited in Africa, it makes sense to try to go beyond this simple label and see how other aspects of the political system essential to democratization are affected by the economic reform process.

LEGAL SYSTEMS THAT MATTER

The first area in which there is an obvious symbiosis between democratic political structures and economic reform is in ensuring property rights through a well-functioning legal system. As noted in chapter 6, an essential part of the PNDC's reform effort has been to convince domestic and foreign investors that there will not be the kind of arbitrary government actions against businessmen or marketwomen that characterized not only the first year of PNDC rule but also previous Ghanaian regimes.[10] That that effort has been less than completely successful is demonstrated by the considerable difficulty the government has had in attracting domestic or foreign investors, except for companies involved in mining. The PNDC must go beyond rhetoric and develop means to reassure potential investors and others that it will not arbitrarily interfere with their economic activities in the future.

The easiest way for the PNDC to establish an environment that

10. The seizure of 50-cedi banknotes by the PNDC as an anticorruption measure in 1982 and the beating of marketwomen was especially harmful to business confidence during the 1980s. The Acheampong regime's seizure of businesses and the Rawlings regime's destruction of Accra's major market in previous years had also suggested that property rights were not guaranteed in Ghana.

promotes business confidence would be to create a legal system that ensures individual economic rights and provides a credible means of resolving conflicts. In Ghana—where for so long the only way to get a foreign exchange license approved, a contract granted, or any type of government service secured was to pay a bribe—the need for the type of assurances provided by a legal system is especially great.

A well-functioning legal system that reassures investors is also an important aspect of democratization. At the most basic level, a functioning legal system can check at least some human rights violations, and its presence constantly reminds soldiers and politicians that they do not have an unhindered field of action in which to pursue their own policy goals or personal enrichment. Also, a well-functioning legal system is a significant departure from the kind of personalistic, patrimonial regimes that many African countries possess. Indeed, a hallmark of these governments is that they are not bound by institutional checks.[11] Finally, a legal system that is able to force public officials to consider public laws is a necessary (although not sufficient) condition for increasing the general accountability of government to the public. Thus, materially and symbolically, moving toward legal systems that matter would be an essential component of any democratization effort that went beyond merely adopting the form of a multiparty system.

Unfortunately, the PNDC, like many other African governments, has yet to construct anything approaching a well-functioning legal system. The government itself, having abrogated the constitution while taking power, is not preoccupied with its legal standing. Although many of the most grievous human rights violations have been halted, this improvement came about because of decisions made by Rawlings rather than strictures from an independent judiciary. In fact, the Ghana Bar Association has been at the forefront of domestic groups criticizing the PNDC throughout the 1980s.[12]

In addition, little thought has been given to what a functional legal system might mean in Ghana. Unfortunately, there is no equivalent to the IMF or the World Bank that might provide the PNDC with a readily usable theory for establishing a credible legal system. Indeed, even international funding for reconstructing the legal system seems difficult to garner.

---

11. This argument is made most strongly by Robert H. Jackson and Carl G. Rosberg, *Personal Rule in Black Africa* (Berkeley: University of California Press, 1982), 1.

12. See, for instance, "Resolutions Passed at the 1988/1989 Annual Conference of the Ghana Bar Association," Accra, Ghana Bar Association, 9 January 1990.

Finally, the PNDC has been notably hostile since its inception to members of the traditional Ghanaian middle class, especially lawyers. Although much of the initial revolutionary energy dissipated as the ERP was enacted, the PNDC retains its strong populist bias against the very people who would have to become more important if the legal system were to matter.

While the PNDC has not instituted legal reform, other African governments might be able to do considerably more. Other African countries will also receive considerable pressure from investors to develop legal systems that matter if their recovery programs are to become self-sustaining. They will also face many of the same difficulties in developing a legal system appropriate to their local conditions. In those other countries, however, there may be considerably less antagonism between the government and the legal profession. Attention and energy need to be devoted to developing legal systems that correspond to the realities and needs of African countries themselves rather than artificially transplanting the facade of Western legal systems. These artificial systems, like the white wigs some African jurists still wear, give the appearance of a legal system, but the laws do not have any roots in the society. If appropriate legal systems could be adopted, there would be a much better chance of political and economic liberalization proceeding concurrently.

THE PRESS

Another important aspect of democratization beyond having a plethora of parties is having a press truly able to convey information to members of the society. As stressed in chapter 6, increasing the flows of information throughout the economy is absolutely essential if economic development is to occur. A press that is relatively free is also important to democratization because accountability cannot be promoted if the public has no idea what the government is doing and if critical voices are not allowed to express their doubts. In Zimbabwe, for example, the *Chronicle*, although government-owned, was instrumental in uncovering a scandal that eventually led to the resignation of five ministers.

But a free press is a radical departure from the kind of closed, authoritarian governments found in so many African countries, including Ghana. Unfortunately, the press in Ghana is far from being free enough to be an important pillar of support for both democratization and economic reform. The electronic media, as in all African countries, are under direct government control and, except for the occasional interview show, are used just to disseminate government press releases. While the two daily newspapers allow for slightly more discussion of public events, they rarely, if ever, print anything that could even be suspected of being critical of the government. Editorials in both papers are seldom more than sycophantic endorsements of government proclamations the previous day. In other words, they are typical African newspapers.

The PNDC seems to have made no effort to reform the press so that it could play a more useful role in Ghanaian society. The reasons are the same as for its unwillingness to strengthen the judiciary: an inability to accept criticism, a fear that loosening of government control over such a key institution would increase the power of "enemies" either inside or outside Ghana, and a preoccupation with other matters. As a result, there is widespread distrust of the newspapers. Many members of the elite, even if they support the PNDC's overall approach, have a derisive attitude toward the daily publications, which report nothing but successes in Ghana.

However, as with legal system reform, it does not appear that the PNDC's failing is inevitable. It is likely that the electronic media, both for technical reasons and because the radio station in particular is seen as a seat of government power in so many African countries, will not be able to escape government control in most countries for the foreseeable future. However, many African countries have the technical ability and a large enough market to allow for private newspapers free from government control. Relatively free private presses in such countries as Zimbabwe and Nigeria demonstrate that there are few technical barriers to a free press if there is no government repression.

PROMOTION OF POLITICAL ASSOCIATIONS

The stress on multiparty structures as the defining aspect of democracy often causes observers to miss the importance of other types of associations that can help citizens digest information and lobby government. Indeed, the usefulness of an improved legal system and freer press will be limited if the polity does not contain vibrant organizations to serve as focal points for political mobilization. For instance, chapter 5 noted that the absence of peasant groups in Ghana similar to those in Zimbabwe meant that opportunities for agrarian producers to influence the policy process and thereby empower themselves were limited. Encouraging political organization outside of parties could simultaneously promote both democratization and economic reform.

The PNDC government has, so far, shown little interest in promoting political organizations, even if they are not in the form of political parties. The top leadership's aversion to how politics was conducted in the past in Ghana has apparently been so powerful that all types of organization are looked upon suspiciously. More generally, it has not been the style of the PNDC to even consult with organizations within Ghana, much less encourage them to form. Thus, despite Ghana's economic resurgence, there has not been a concomitant increase in organizations that might transmit important information to the government apparatus about developments in the economy.

In addition, the multilateral organizations, which play such an important part in decision making in Ghana, do not seem to have any particular interest in encouraging political organizations. Indeed, given the IMF and World Bank's limited presence on the ground in African countries, a plethora of local political organizations that would have to be consulted would probably only make the multilaterals' job, at least in their own eyes, more difficult. Thus, the multilaterals and secretive African governments tend to mutually reinforce the barriers to private political organizations having an institutionalized presence during policy formation.

Once again, the unwillingness of the PNDC to allow political organizations to increase participation in the policy process as reform continues does not mean that other countries could not allow political organizations to become more important. As chapter 5 makes clear, the lack of such participation hinders efforts to promote agriculture. Countries truly committed to enhancing their agrarian sectors might therefore be more inclined to let political organizations, including groups representing peasants, operate openly in the country. Indeed, elections alone probably will not cause peasants to gain a share of political power concomitant with their demographic weight. Peasants also need the ability to organize so that they can block roads, demonstrate openly, and march to cities to constantly remind politicians of their overwhelming numbers. Indeed, increasing participation in the political process by important economic actors is clearly one of the concrete aspects of the highly speculative relationship between political and economic liberalization.

Reforms of the legal system, enhancing the freedom of the press, and allowing political organizations to represent economic actors are all elements of democratization. They are in many ways as important as adopting a system of multiparty elections. Indeed, while free and fair elections would have an important impact, they can just as easily result in the kind of political and economic chaos that characterized countries such as Ghana and Nigeria during their civilian regimes.

Positive developments in all three areas would also promote economic development. A functioning legal system, a free press, and the presence of political associations would be helpful to the structural adjustment phase of economic reform. New investment, the ultimate goal of the structural adjustment phase, will occur only if property rights are protected. In addition, as stressed in chapter 6, a crucial aspect of structural adjustment is that enough information be transmitted throughout the economy that economic decision makers can make well-grounded decisions. Indeed, reform in these three areas is probably more consequential to promoting economic activity in the short term than is simply holding elections.

Furthermore, in African countries, meaningful electoral systems adapted to local circumstances will also take time to develop, especially given the previous failures. Reforms of the legal system, press, and political organizations, however, can proceed more quickly. First, reforms in this area can be implemented incrementally and do not engender the same kind of uncertainty that instituting a whole new electoral system would. Also, reforms in these areas will not threaten the leadership of a country as much as will instituting a multiparty system, so politicians are more likely to adopt them quickly.

Thus, the relationship between democratization and economic reform needs to be reexamined at a less abstract level. There is no reason to believe that reform will be promoted simply because a country adopts a political system in which there is electoral competition. Indeed, if there are not significant reforms in the legal system, press freedoms, and the ability of political organizations to pressure the government, there may be little relationship between political reforms and improvements in the national economy. Certainly, this was the case with Ghana's previous civilian regime. Conversely, if reforms are made in the areas noted above, there can be a significant positive association between political liberalization and economic reform.

THE POTENTIAL FOR INSTITUTIONALIZING REFORM

Clearly, the question of regime choice will not be settled in most African countries for a considerable time. Therefore, especially given the turbulence in African politics and the number of countries undergoing fundamental changes, an important question is whether or not economic reforms begun by certain types of regimes can be institutionalized. This question also impinges on many of the problems noted in chapter 1 concerning the origin and functioning of institutions. As North noted, the exact relationship between ideas and relative prices during times of regime change is unclear. This in-depth study of Ghana provides some conclusions regarding the future of the African state and the specific issues raised by the "new institutionalism."

One way of approaching the problem of institutional change is to ask which factors lead to permanent reform. This question is particularly important given the number of regime changes occurring across Africa. Reforms that involve fundamental changes in institutions are more likely to continue, especially compared to the fragility of simple price reform. Successor governments can alter prices of foreign exchange, of goods, or of labor with relatively little problem if the process of setting prices has not changed. Thus, the Ghanaian reform of the exchange rate probably could not have been said to be institutionalized until the government established the auction.

In addition, changing fundamental institutions establishes certain foci around which proreform constituencies can coalesce over the long term. Indeed, given that the immediate benefits of reform will be limited and that, as argued in chapter 8, many of the beneficiaries of reforms will not recognize themselves as such for a considerable time, establishing institutions around which those in favor of reform will slowly coalesce will be particularly important.

Another important aspect of the reform process is the changes in the incentives posed by the international system. Previously, as North and Thomas argue, fear of being conquered by other states has often impelled leaders to improve the functioning of their national political and economic systems.[13] African states today do not face that particular risk. Indeed, African states have made a considerable effort to establish a regime to promote boundary stability, and there are few African countries at present with the capability to attack, much less overrun, their neighbors. As a result, even extremely weak African states continue to exist.[14]

However, throughout the 1980s, the costs of economic failure have risen. The increasing conditionality of all aid from multilateral and

13. Douglass C. North and Robert Paul Thomas, *The Rise of the Western World* (Cambridge: Cambridge University Press, 1973), 80–81.
14. See Jeffrey Herbst, "War and the State in Africa," *International Security* 14, no. 4 (Spring 1990).

bilateral donors has meant that countries that performed poorly, such as
pre-1983 Ghana, received less aid. Also, with the end of the cold war, the
United States in particular has moved away from strategic considerations and begun to base increasing amounts of its aid on progress in
economic reform. For example, traditional strategic allies but poor reformers such as Zaire, Liberia, and Sudan have received relatively less
money. Clearly, this trend will continue in the future.

At the same time, the international community has increased the
rewards for reform. The large amount of money available in the various
World Bank and IMF facilities as well as the willingness of bilateral
donors such as the United States to shift money to good performers has
increased the attractiveness of reform to leaders. More generally, the end
of the cold war has made it clear that countries will increasingly compete
against each other on the basis of economic performance (as opposed to,
for example, strategic location), and those countries that reform fastest
will, like Ghana, receive a large amount of aid for their efforts. Clearly,
the rise of first the East Asian countries and then the Southeast Asian
countries has only emphasized to African countries that they are being
marginalized and that they will only fall further behind if they do not
reform now.

Thus, there has been a clear shift in the incentives that leaders face
when trying to make calculations about politically difficult reforms.
While the new set of rewards and sanctions facing African leaders may
not be as powerful as the threat of territorial conquest, leaders such as
Rawlings who are willing to change fundamental rules in their countries
may be attracted to the reform agenda. In the long term, this argument is
probably more persuasive than examining the success such organizations as the World Bank have had imposing particular conditions. Indeed, many specific conditions imposed by the multilaterals have not
been met.[15] However, over time, the incentives facing leaders have significantly changed with the result that there is now a much greater likelihood of reform than in the past.

If simply the intellectual climate regarding the economic role of the
state had changed, it is doubtful if Ghana would have adopted such a
radical reform program or if so many other African countries would be
attempting to duplicate its success. As noted repeatedly throughout this
book, while the ideas associated with structural adjustment provide a

15. See Paul Mosley, Jane Harrigan, and John Toye, *Aid and Power,* vol. 1: *The World
Bank and Policy-Based Lending* (New York: Routledge, 1991), chap. 5.

compelling critique of previous state practices, they do not, by themselves, suggest a viable strategy for reform or a new set of political institutions appropriate for a reformed political economy. It is up to individual African governments to develop these new strategies and institutions. For instance, the PNDC was successful in devising strategies for initial price reform but less adept at creating conditions for sustained changes in fundamental institutions.

Given the perils of structural adjustment, it is clear that the new orthodoxy guiding development thinking in the 1980s and 1990s was not a sufficient influence by itself to cause so many African governments to change basic political practices. Rather, the fundamental alteration of the incentives that African leaders receive from the international system in terms of the cost of economic failure seems to have been more consequential. If the multilaterals and the individual aid agencies had not become tougher on poor economic performers while providing large sums to those countries that did reform, the new intellectual orthodoxy would not have been enough.

As was noted in chapter 7, however, the multilaterals have a significant comparative advantage in promoting some reforms over others. Price reforms are easily observable to organizations that have a limited presence in a country, and they are especially important given that economists dominate the IMF and the World Bank. Conversely, the multilaterals have difficulty observing the long-term process of reforming institutions and may have less to contribute to the overall reform process. Thus, pressure from the multilaterals may cause African countries to continually attempt to correct prices even if they are not successful in the much larger and more important project of adjusting basic institutions. African states would therefore be caught in a trap, constantly trying to correct prices that are continually being thrown into disequilibrium because of government inability to change the way in which the underlying institutions determine the prices. For instance, a government that continued to determine the exchange rate administratively rather than devolving authority to the market could face continual devaluation crises.

Clearly, a large number of factors interact to determine when a government decides to begin reform measures and how successful those reforms will be. However, the Ghana case does indicate that some types of reform will probably be easier to institutionalize than others. In addition, it is important to recognize that the international environment has fundamentally changed. In the 1990s, a government that fails to reform will not simply be able to revert to 1970s-style stagnation. There will be continual pressure on governments to at least stabilize their economies. However, the attempts by international actors to make sure that governments reform fundamental institutions will inevitably be less successful. As stressed throughout this book, unless African governments themselves develop strategies and political structures concomitant with the tasks implied by structural adjustment, there will be very little help that international actors can offer.

THE POWER OF THE AFRICAN STATE

As the reform process continues in African countries, a more nuanced view of the ability of African states may evolve. It has become something of a cottage industry to enumerate the weaknesses of the African state.[16] Indeed, given the decay that African states have experienced, many would agree with Young and Turner when they argue that the state "risks becoming an irrelevancy."[17] Of course, states in Africa are, on average, far weaker than most states across the world: They are impoverished; their administrative reach does not extend beyond the capital; and their revenue sources are erratic. In addition, there are increasing claims that various organizations within society can fulfill some of the tasks once thought to be the province of the state.[18] At the very least, there is now the belief that societal organizations actually flourish when the center is moribund.[19] More generally, the power of organizations within African societies has been emphasized while the capabilities of the state have been overlooked.

However, African states retain the power to set many of the rules by which the political system and the economy operate. In a previous work I referred to this capacity as "structural autonomy."[20] For instance, the Ghanaian government, despite its evident weaknesses in the early 1980s,

16. See, for instance, Robert H. Jackson and Carl G. Rosberg, "The Marginality of African States," in *African Independence: The First Twenty-Five Years,* ed. Gwendolen M. Carter and Patrick O'Meara (Bloomington: Indiana University Press, 1985).

17. Crawford Young and Thomas Turner, *The Rise and Decline of the Zairian State* (Madison: University of Wisconsin Press, 1985), 45.

18. Victor Azarya, "Reordering State-Society Relations: Incorporation and Disengagement," in *The Precarious Balance: State and Society in Africa,* ed. Naomi Chazan and Donald Rothchild (Boulder: Westview, 1988), 8.

19. Naomi Chazan, "Ghana: Problems of Governance and the Emergence of Civil Society," in *Democracy in Developing Countries: Africa,* ed. Larry Diamond, Juan J. Linz, and Seymour Martin Lipset (Boulder: Lynne Rienner, 1988), 130.

20. Jeffrey Herbst, *State Politics in Zimbabwe* (Berkeley: University of California Press, 1990).

was still able to devalue and to lift price controls. These actions had an enormous impact on the economy and affected a large number of people. A perhaps more important point when examining the power of the state, the PNDC's extensive reforms of the exchange rate and price controls have meant that, over relatively few years, the government has fundamentally changed the politics of allocation. By devaluing, lifting price controls, and eliminating other aspects of state policy that had encouraged rent seeking, the PNDC has removed past incentives to try to gain economic advantage through the state and has encouraged private sector activity. Indeed, the state's juridical ability to change fundamental aspects of the political economy is often ignored by those who concentrate solely on the African state's weaknesses.

The fixation on state weakness also causes analysts to ignore that it was often the state's own self-defeating economic policies that caused its weakness. The Ghanaian state, like many others in Africa, had to devote so much manpower to tasks such as foreign exchange allocation or price control that it could not attend to more traditional state matters. Also, the fact that the state was making so many important economic decisions almost invariably invited corruption. Thus, the weak African state is not an inevitable product of local circumstances or colonialism but, at least in part, is the result of government policies that inadvertently accentuated those areas where the state is weakest.

Reform programs, by devolving some economic decisions to the market, allow resources to be redirected so the state can become stronger. For instance, the administrative allocation of ever-scarcer foreign exchange posed far greater operational challenges to the government than did devaluation. Similarly, the flow of external funds into Ghana has helped strengthen the administrative apparatus by promoting training and enhancing institutional structures. Thus, just as African states became weaker while they expanded their scope, retrenchment allows them to address more competently the tasks they still have to fulfill.

The ability of even weak states to fundamentally alter the political economy of African countries has been ignored for several reasons. First, many scholars have assumed a correlation between the degree to which a reform (e.g., devaluation) is politically controversial and the administrative difficulty involved in implementing the measure. In fact, once a government is committed to devaluation, it is easier to implement than is usually thought. The Ghanaian government was also able to institute first the auction and then the legalization of foreign bureaus with relatively little difficulty. Ghana was able to rely on the multilateral organizations, especially the IMF, for the administrative expertise it lacked.

Second, there has been considerable confusion on how economic decline affects the state-society balance of power. It is true that during decline, alternative organizations appear. For instance, if the state distorts prices enough, black markets will eventually allocate goods. Thus, in Ghana, almost all goods were being distributed on the black market by the early 1980s. However, black marketeers are dependent on the presence of state policies that distort the economy. Once these distorted policies are removed, illegal markets disappear because there is a considerable loss associated with black marketeering. For instance, cocoa smuggling to Côte d'Ivoire decreased markedly once the Ghanaian Cocoa Board raised the prices it paid to farmers.

Despite much having been written about the growth of associational life in Africa during the process of state disintegration, it is probably not the case that other social organizations become unambiguously more powerful as the state declines. What little systematic evidence there is suggests that associational life is not particularly evident in Ghana, despite the long period of decline the country experienced. In 1988, as part of its health and demographic survey, the government of Ghana and the Institute for Resource Development asked 4,488 women what organizations they belonged to. The results, while tentative, do not indicate an explosion of social organizations. Only 9.4 percent belonged to social organizations, 5.5 percent to financial, and 3.7 percent to occupational.[21] Indeed, the only truly significant societal organizations that women report they belong to are religious organizations (24.1 percent) that, although they may offer solace in times of economic and political decay, predate Ghana's economic decline. A mere 0.7 percent belonged to "other" groups.

Anecdotal evidence suggests that societal organizations were as badly affected by the long-term economic crisis as was the state. With no money for fuel or spare parts to operate cars, a disintegrating telephone system, and shortages of paper, it was hard for many organizations just to reach their members. The necessity for everyone to work two or three jobs simply to earn a minimal living also severely hurt the vitality of societal organizations. While the state may have been declining faster than other societal organizations, it is clear that during the 1970s and early 1980s every organization in Ghana was falling apart. Thus, the

21. Institute for Resource Development, unpublished data.

belief, increasingly prevalent in the literature, that societal organizations can somehow replace the functions that the state traditionally performs, should be questioned.

Indeed, as stressed in chapters 3 and 4, the state was able to implement the difficult stabilization measures in part because almost all organizations in Ghana had collapsed. When the government finally announced its policy reforms, there were no obvious organizations or fronts that people opposed to the new policies could rally around. Instead, given the institutional vacuum, whatever opposition there was could emerge only through spontaneous uprisings. However, as noted in chapter 4, the PNDC had the ability to repress these minor protests. The government was also determined enough that it could shed the support of those few organizations (e.g., the labor unions) with the potential to provide some kind of organized opposition.

Rather than economic and political decline causing the state to lose freedom of action to associational groups, the absence of coherent organizations in society may aid a "soft" state that has adopted a reform program. Regimes in countries that have not experienced as dramatic a decline as Ghana may face more vibrant opposition because those opposed to the new policies will be able to coalesce around relatively strong societal groups. While economic decline does not automatically lead to reform programs being adopted, particularly weak states do have some advantages, especially considering the strength of their opponents, should they decide to adopt dramatic new policies.

In addition, rather than increasing as the state and economy decline, societal organizations prosper when the economy is relatively sound. As Michael Bratton has noted, societal organizations are strongest in countries—such as South Africa, Kenya, and Zimbabwe—where there has been the greatest economic development outside the state.[22] Societal organizations will be most prevalent where there are more free-floating resources they can garner. Thus, economic reform programs that promote economic growth will engender an environment where associational groups can prosper.

CONCLUSION

The fate of literally tens of millions of people rests on the success of economic and political reform programs in Africa. Questions of state

22. Michael Bratton, "Beyond the State: Civil Society and Associational Life in Africa," *World Politics* 41, no. 4 (April 1990): 427.

ability, regime type, and the relationship between political and economic reform are not merely academic but critical to the fate of a continent. The Ghanaian case demonstrates that all these issues should be approached with intellectual modesty because so many had written off Ghana as hopeless by the early 1980s. Africa's most successful reformer demonstrates that there is hope for much of the continent—assuming policymakers and international organizations approach with nuance and finesse the difficult issues of political and economic reform. It is to be hoped that other African countries will join Ghana in suggesting just how wrong the conventional view is.

Index

Compositor: Keystone Typesetting, Inc.
Text: 10/13 Sabon
Display: Sabon
Printer: BookCrafters, Inc.
Binder: BookCrafters, Inc.